THE INTEGRATION OF THE PACIFIC COAST LEAGUE

THE INTEGRATION OF THE
PACIFIC COAST LEAGUE

RACE AND BASEBALL ON THE WEST COAST

AMY ESSINGTON

University of Nebraska Press
Lincoln and London

Parts of chapters 3–5 were originally published in
"Equality on the Baseball Diamond: Integrating the
Pacific Coast League, 1948–1952," *Journal of the West*
47, no. 4 (Fall 2008). © 2008 by ABC-CLIO, LLC.
Reprinted with permission of ABC-CLIO, LLC.

Library of Congress Cataloging-in-Publication Data
Names: Essington, Amy, author.
Title: The integration of the Pacific Coast League: race
and baseball on the West Coast / Amy Essington.
Description: Lincoln: University of Nebraska Press,
2018. | Includes bibliographical references and index.
Identifiers: LCCN 2017043081
ISBN 9780803285736 (paperback: alk. paper)
ISBN 9781496207074 (epub)
ISBN 9781496207081 (mobi)
ISBN 9781496207098 (pdf)
Subjects: LCSH: Pacific Coast League—History—20th
century. | Baseball—Pacific States—History—20th
century. | Discrimination in sports—Pacific States. |
Discrimination in sports—United States. | Baseball—
United States—History. | BISAC: SPORTS &
RECREATION / Baseball / History. | SOCIAL SCIENCE
/ Ethnic Studies / African American Studies.
| HISTORY / United States / State & Local /
West (AK, CA, CO, HI, ID, MT, NV, UT, WY).
Classification: LCC GV875.P33 E77 2018 |
DDC 796.3570979—dc23
LC record available at https://lccn.loc.gov/2017043081

Set in Lyon by Mikala R Kolander.
Designed by N. Putens.

For Ian

CONTENTS

ILLUSTRATIONS

ACKNOWLEDGMENTS

In many ways this book began with Effa Manley, co-owner of the Newark Eagles and 2006 Baseball Hall of Fame inductee. A white woman who chose to live her life as an African American, Manley challenged racial and gender roles throughout her life. Her story led me to the Negro Leagues and then to the integration of baseball. My interest in integration grew the summer I worked as an intern in the library at the National Baseball Hall of Fame. A native Californian, I was always in search of material about baseball on the West Coast. I combined my interest in integration and my desire to learn more about baseball on the West Coast and began researching the integration of the Pacific Coast League (PCL). As I explain in the introduction, it was a more difficult prospect than I had originally thought it would be.

Many people have helped me during the process of writing this book. First, thank you to Janet Farrell Brodie, Samuel O. Regalado, and Jack Schuster. Their patience and encouragement helped me continue to move forward even as the years passed. Their knowledge and critiques helped me produce a better product. I would like to include a special note about Jules Tygiel. He passed away in 2008, before I completed the project. His contributions to this field of history were numerous, and this book would not have been possible without his work.

Many people helped me with research and finding material, including Dick Beverage, the former president of the Pacific Coast League Historical Society; Eric Enders and Tim Wiles at the National Baseball Hall of Fame; and the members of the local chapters of the Society for American Baseball Research (SABR) in California, Oregon, and Washington. A special thank-you to Bill Swank, who connected me with John Ritchey's notebook and his widow, Lydia. This manuscript has been improved by the work at the University of Nebraska Press of Rob Taylor, senior acquisitions editor; Courtney Ochsner, associate acquisitions editor; and Annette Wenda, copyeditor.

On a personal level I would like to thank friends and relatives who let me stay with them during research trips, including Caroline Castaneda, Craig and Mitzi Elsten, and Renee and Kurt Rupe. Thank you to Dee Abrahamse for reading chapters multiple times. I would also like to thank Lara Godbille; Laurie Richlin; my in-laws, Jim Welke and Barbara Wood; and my parents, John and Patricia Essington, for their support. Most of all, I wish to thank Ian Welke, who knew before I did that we would make a good team.

THE INTEGRATION OF THE PACIFIC COAST LEAGUE

INTRODUCTION

This is a story about individuals who wanted to play a game they loved, baseball. For many years the game denied some of these players access to the sport because of their race. With pressure from the outside, the power structure changed, and those previously denied finally had the opportunity to prove their skills as professional baseball players. This book examines the integration of the Pacific Coast League, a minor baseball league in the three states along the Pacific Coast, from 1903 to 1957. While the PCL was not the first Minor League to integrate (that milestone went to the International League in 1946), it was the first league in baseball, at either the Minor or the Major League level, to have each of its teams include a player of color on its roster during the regular season. The integration of the PCL happened over five seasons, from 1948 to 1952. I began this project with the name of each player who integrated each PCL team. It became important to me to compile a full story of which players joined what teams and when and also to examine the process of integration in the PCL.

This is the first work to examine the integration of a Minor League. In *Brushing Back Jim Crow: The Integration of Minor League Baseball in the American South* (1999), Bruce Adelson examined the integration of Minor Leagues in the South, but he focused on a region of the country, not on any particular league in the South. When we understand integration in a specific league, the roles of individuals in the process of integration become more apparent. By defining who decided when a team or a league would segregate and who decided when they would integrate, we can learn much about racism and the process of integration. In studying Major League Baseball (MLB), the answer to the first part of the question is usually Cap Anson, a player-manager who refused to play against African Americans in the 1880s, and the answer to the second part of the question is Branch Rickey, the president of the Brooklyn Dodgers, who signed Jackie Robinson to a professional baseball contract in 1945. The experiences of these two individuals, who are well known to integration history, do not tell the whole story. Integration was a process that involved hundreds of players on dozens of teams in tens of leagues across the country and over decades. If the story of integration ends with Jackie Robinson and Branch Rickey, we lose the story that happened to everyone beyond those two men and the larger understanding of integration in sport as part of the social movement for civil rights that grew and developed during and after World War II.

The story of integration goes beyond the Major Leagues. The Minor Leagues are an important aspect of baseball history in general and integration history specifically that baseball historians have ignored in favor of the Major Leagues. While histories of Jackie Robinson note that he spent a year with the Montreal Royals, a Minor League team of the Brooklyn Dodgers, the hundreds of other players of color who followed him onto the rosters of Minor Leagues throughout the country have not yet been studied comprehensively. Professional baseball included a system of Minor Leagues for each Major League team. Without the integration of the Minor Leagues, integration of the Major Leagues would not have been possible. Despite their previous professional experience in the Negro Leagues, most players of color were sent to Minor League teams before moving to the Major League rosters. Even if they had the experience to play at the Major League level, players of color usually went into the Minors before joining a Major League team.

In the history of the integration of professional baseball, Branch Rickey and Jackie Robinson have been the focus of many studies. As pioneers on the forefront of social change, their actions should be recognized and studied. However, Robinson was one of hundreds of players who integrated professional baseball. Jackie Robinson was not even the only African American on the 1946 Montreal Royals' roster or the 1947 Brooklyn Dodgers' roster. The Brooklyn Dodgers were not the only Major League team with players of color on the roster in 1947; Larry Doby joined the Cleveland Indians on July 5, 1947, and for that season he was the only black player on the Indians. Hank Thompson joined the St. Louis Browns on July 17, 1947, and was joined by Willard Brown two days later. The Major Leagues were not the only level in baseball with integrated teams. In 1946, in addition to the league in which Jackie Robinson played, the Triple-A International League and three other leagues—the New England League, the Canadian-American League, and the Border League—included African Americans. In 1947 two additional leagues, the Sunset League and the Colonial League, joined those four. The study of the integration of baseball should recognize the role of Jackie Robinson but not focus on the career of one pioneer. With a focus on the players in the West and in recognition of the hundreds of players across professional baseball who integrated teams, this book attempts to expand the historical focus from one man to many, and thus I will limit my discussion about Jackie Robinson.

Integration did not occur in a vacuum but happened based on geographic location and social influences in the region in which it occurred. The racial experience in the West differed from that of other regions of the country. The structure of racism and discrimination in the West was not as rigid or as prescribed by law as in other areas. With African Americans, Asian Americans, Latinos, and Native Americans all living in the West, racial and ethnic relations spanned a more complex map than the simpler black-white dichotomy in other regions of the United States. During the establishment of territories and creation of states in the West, which included a more diverse population, many western communities established complex patterns of segregation and discrimination, frequently with more flexible rules than other areas of the country. The leagues in the West distinguished among different minority groups and restricted some of them, while allowing others to play. Over time African Americans, light-skinned and dark-skinned Latinos, Native Americans, and a limited number of Asian Americans all joined both Major and Minor League teams. The difference was that in the West, the communities in which the teams existed were more diverse. Players of color in the West could expect to find that their local communities of African Americans, Asian Americans, or Latinos supported and rooted for them at the games. While the population of African Americans was larger in other regions of the country, the West had a greater multiplicity of racial groups. While states in the West may have discriminated against all minority groups, the PCL seemed to limit its segregation to those whom others defined as black.

Why did integration happen after World War II? The integration of baseball in particular, and sports in general, happened as part of the long and wide civil rights movement. Years of activism by African Americans combined with millions of service members returning home from a war in which they fought for freedom and democracy challenged a society that did not treat them equally. As works like *An American Dilemma* (1944) by Gunnar Myrdal brought the discussion of race to the forefront of American society, the death of Major League Baseball commissioner Kenesaw Mountain Landis, who worked to oppose integration, brought new leadership to the power structure of professional baseball. The foundation of activism combined with lessons from war and helped create a postwar society ready for change.

Several books claim that a team or league integrated before professional baseball did so in 1946. There are examples of players who may or may not have claimed to be African American whom some will cite as the ones who integrated a team or a league. In *The California Winter League: America's First Integrated Professional Baseball League* (2002), William F. McNeil argues that the California Winter League was integrated. In the Winter League all-black teams played against all-white teams. While this system allowed blacks on Negro League teams to display their skills against whites, it was not integrated. The players did not play together; they played against one another. In another book, *Color Blind: The Forgotten Team That Broke Baseball's Color Line* (2013), Tom Dunkel examines a semiprofessional baseball team in Bismarck, North Dakota, in the 1930s. While this team did include black and white players on the same roster, it was a semiprofessional team and therefore not part of formal organized baseball.[1] I argue that one individual playing for a single team sometime in a single game is not integration. Integration is a sustained movement for social change and requires more than one person.

Those who held the power to decide to segregate or to integrate the sport of baseball were the owners of the teams. The owners of the Pacific Coast League teams left little to no documentary evidence of their views regarding segregation or integration. Six of the eight teams had the same owner or majority owner throughout the 1948–52 period. They included William "Bill" Starr, who purchased the San Diego Padres in 1944; Philip K. Wrigley, who inherited the Los Angeles Angels, the team his father bought in 1921; Robert H. "Bob" Cobb and a group of other Hollywood figures, who purchased the Hollywood Stars in 1939; Clarence "Brick" Laws, who became owner of the Oakland Oaks in 1943; George Norgan, who co-owned the Portland Beavers with William Klepper from 1943 to 1946 and became the sole owner of the team from 1946 to 1954; and Emil G. Sick, owner of the Seattle Rainiers from 1937. The San Francisco Seals, owned since 1921 by Charles Graham Sr. and co-owned by Graham with Paul Fagan from 1946, was owned exclusively by Fagan from 1950. The Sacramento Solons had a group of owners who co-owned the 2,500 shares of stock. Yubi G. Separovich was the majority shareholder until Oscar Salenger brought 53 percent of the stock shares in 1948. In 1951 Eddie Mulligan purchased the team. He retained majority ownership until 1955.

This collection of owners left almost no records of either opinions about the process of integration or opinions about any individual player, except what appears in newspaper stories. As I discuss in chapter 2, Bill Starr makes no mention of John Ritchey or integration in his book *Clearing the Bases: Baseball Then and Now* (1998). No other PCL owner authored a book. The minutes of the annual meetings of the directors from 1943 to 1954 do not include one reference to integration or any race-related issues.[2] The minutes do not include any reference to the tryouts in 1943, the signing of Jackie Robinson or any other player of color to a Major League team, or the signing of John Ritchey or any other player of color to a Minor League team in the PCL. Whether the PCL owners had the ability to choose to sign a Major League player may be indicated in the response of owners to two situations unrelated to integration. In 1943, as part of a discussion about the Committee for Patriotic Programs, Seattle Rainiers owner Emil Sick expressed a concern about losing players if the U.S. government stopped baseball for the duration of World War II. Hollywood Stars owner Victor Collins replied that the PCL Board of Directors could not pass a resolution that disapproved of the rules of Major League Baseball.[3] While the comment by Collins may have been about the perception of the league's patriotism, it also indicated that the league was part of a larger organization. It would appear from this statement that a Minor League owner could not have signed a player of color before a Major League owner did.

A second remark in the minutes of the Board of Directors meeting came from the man who signed the first African American to a PCL team. In 1948 San Diego Padres owner Bill Starr said, "I am sure that none of us can stop progress and if the people demand television, we are going to give it to them.... If we take a reactionary attitude, they won't come out to the ballpark."[4] Starr commented on the future of the PCL and television, but the statement came just two months after John Ritchey joined the Padres. Maybe Starr understood the meaning of progress on several levels and that owners should react to what the fans wanted.

The decision to integrate a baseball team had positive financial consequences. In 1947, in his regular *Los Angeles Sentinel* column, "Abie's Corner," Edward "Abie" Robinson proposed that the PCL could increase their attendance at games if teams signed black players. "Our famed president [Clarence "Pants" Rowland] can't see the coming of the Negro in baseball. There are 10,000 Negro baseball fans here in Los Angeles who would easily become daily patrons of Wrigley Field, within a stone's throw of the heart of the Negro community."[5] When a PCL team roster included players of color, attendance increased. On June 2, 1949, attendance at PCL games was 1.25 million, an increase of 17,494 over the previous year. San Diego had an increase in attendance from 424,200 in 1948 to 493,780 in 1949.[6] One reason was Luke Easter and his ability to hit home runs.[7] When Easter injured his knee, PCL owners complained that the loss of the home run hitter in the lineup cost them $200,000.[8] The financial success that Luke Easter provided for the San Diego Padres inspired others to integrate as well.

A NOTE ABOUT SOURCES

I began this project with a list. In the *Pacific Coast League Trivia Book: Facts about Fabulous Feats and Foolishness, 1903-1957* (1997), John Spalding includes a list called "Color Barriers Busters."[9] With a short introduction about Jimmy Claxton and Artie Wilson and the integration of Oakland Oaks, Spalding lists each PCL team, the integrating player and his position, and the year of integration. The only specific date included is when John Ritchey integrated the San Diego Padres on March 30, 1948.

With this list I went to the Pacific Coast League Historical Society in Placentia, California, and spoke with its president, Richard Beverage. He informed me that the PCL did not have any extant archives. His story included a move back East, the back of a truck opening on the highway, and the loss of records. The California Historical Society holds the most extensive collection on the PCL, the Dick Dobbins Collection on the Pacific Coast League, 1866–1999. The collection focuses on the years 1903–57 and includes material not found elsewhere, such as minutes from PCL board meetings and tapes of oral histories completed by Dick Dobbins, including John and Lydia Ritchey, Artie Wilson, and William "Barney" or "Bonnie" Serrell. I spent a summer working in the National Baseball Hall of Fame Library, so I came to know their collection. While there were a few vertical files about teams of the PCL or its players, the information focused on time spent on Major League teams, if applicable. When I worked there the library did not subscribe to any West Coast newspapers, nor had they ever, to my knowledge. With incomplete league records, I then searched for team records for each of the eight teams during the period of integration, finding only partial records for the Seattle Rainiers at the Washington State Historical Society.

Next, moving on to the people who participated in the integration of the PCL, many of the important figures were already deceased and had not left personal records. None of the owners or managers is currently alive, and only one of the players who integrated the teams is alive. Player obituaries focused on the teams and statistics of a player. The only PCL team owner to author a book was Bill Starr, owner of the San Diego Padres. In *Clearing the Bases: Baseball Now and Then* (1998), he makes no mention of integration. The only PCL player of color to have written an autobiography is Minnie Miñoso, and he wrote two, *Extra Innings: My Life in Baseball* (1983) and *Just Call Me Minnie: My Six Decades in Baseball* (1994). No biographies exist of any of the owners or players. Biographies of two PCL managers during the period of integration, Lefty O'Doul and Rogers Hornsby, only briefly reference race, but the comments are not related to the integration of the PCL teams.[10]

In each PCL team city I checked historical societies as possible sources. The San Diego Historical Society has a few vertical files on the city's African Americans, but they focus on the 1960s. I did find an oral history interview of Bert Ritchey, the brother of John Ritchey, who integrated the San Diego

Padres. The California Room of the San Diego Central Library contains some vertical files related to housing and school integration, but, again, it centers on the 1960s and later. San Diego State University has microfilm of the *Aztec*, the school newspaper, which includes articles about John Ritchey.

The Central Branch of the Los Angeles Public Library has a few vertical files relating to baseball, but not about the integration of the PCL. The Paul Ziffren Sports Resource Center of the Amateur Athletic Foundation of Los Angeles has collections of *Baseball Digest*, *Baseball Magazine*, *Sporting Life*, and *The Sporting News*, the major publication about baseball during the period of integration. The availability of these periodicals has proved useful.

The Oakland History Room of the city's public library provided limited information about the PCL, but nothing about integration. The African American Museum and Library at Oakland has a great collection of material on the Oakland Larks, the city's Negro League team in 1946, but limited information in a few vertical files about integration and the Oakland Oaks. The Main Library of the San Francisco Public Library includes a San Francisco History Center and an African American History Center with a few references to the PCL. In Sacramento the California Room of the California State Archives, the California State Library, and the Sacramento City Library produced only a few references to the PCL, in general.

In the Pacific Northwest the Oregon Historical Society has a picture of blacks playing baseball, but not related to integration and not of much use to my research. The Central Library of Multnomah County offers some vertical files, but not any specific to the PCL. The Black Resource Center at the North Public Library of Multnomah County has a number of copies of local secondary works about African Americans in Portland and Oregon. The Central Branch of the Seattle Public Library has a few vertical files, but not related to the integration of the PCL. The African American Collection at the Douglass-Truth Branch of the Seattle Public Library has copies of secondary works related to African Americans in Seattle. The Washington State Historical Society in Tacoma has the only records in the area related to the Seattle Rainiers.

The sources that were most readily available and useful were newspapers. The *Los Angeles Times*, *Chicago Defender*, *Los Angeles Sentinel*, and *San Francisco Chronicle* (before 1922) were available and searchable in ProQuest.

The *San Diego Union, San Diego Tribune, Oakland Tribune, San Francisco Chronicle* (after 1922), *Portland Tribune,* and *Seattle Times,* all of the major newspapers from the cities with PCL teams, are available only on microfilm and usually only in the city of publication. National black papers such as the *Chicago Defender* and *Baltimore Afro-American* also included news from the West Coast, but focused on the East, especially the integration of the Major Leagues more than the Minor Leagues. The *Los Angeles Sentinel* did include coverage of the Pacific Coast League, including integration, but focused on black players and not Asian Americans.

A number of local researchers connected me to information about the players of the PCL. In particular, author and local historian Bill Swank in San Diego introduced me to the widow and nephew of John Ritchey, both of whom I interviewed. I also interviewed a white teammate of John Ritchey. The interview demonstrates the difficulty of getting direct answers about race in the past. I had been told that Ritchey's teammate was opposed to integration when it happened, but during the interview the player talked of supporting it. Since the interview did not furnish any useful information related to integration, I will not name the player. Swank also provided me with a valuable resource, a copy of John Ritchey's personal scrapbook. The Ritcheys collected the articles in the scrapbook during his baseball-playing days, and it includes newspaper articles from junior high, high school, college, the Negro Leagues, and the PCL. John Ritchey and his family members clipped and collected the articles as he played. The articles are not in exact chronological order, and they are not dated. Most do not have the source of the articles. I have been able to identify some of the newspapers and dates, but only a handful. It is a very valuable resource in that it details the whole career of Ritchey.

Other useful sources have been the oral histories conducted and published by others, particularly those done with players from the Negro Leagues. Books such as John Holway's *Voice from the Great Black Baseball Leagues* (1992) and Brent Kelley's *Voices from the Negro Leagues: Conversations with 52 Baseball Standouts* (2000), *The Negro Leagues Revisited: Conversations with 66 More Baseball Heroes* (2000), and *"I Will Never Forget": Interviews with 39 Former Negro League Players* (2003) all provide firsthand accounts of Negro League players, some of whom integrated Major or Minor League teams. Books that have interviews with PCL players include *Echoes from Lane Field: A History of the San Diego Padres* (1999), *Nuggets on the Diamond: Professional Baseball in the Bay Area from the Gold Rush to the Present* (1994), and *The Grand Minor League: An Oral History of the Old Pacific Coast League* (1999).[11]

Overall, I found it difficult to find primary sources about my subject other than newspaper articles. Baseball is a sport with a detailed history, but one that focuses on numbers and statistics rather than the personal lives of players. With most of the players deceased, the oral histories completed by others become even more valuable.

TERMINOLOGY

In sport history the process of signing players of color to a previously all-white team has been called integration. I believe that the term *integration* does not accurately reflect the process of what really happened. *Integration* would imply that a player of color had full access to everything that the white player did within the game. Black and Latino players of the 1940s and 1950s could not always eat at the same restaurants or stay in the same hotels as their white teammates. When they could stay at the same hotel, players of color did not room with white players, and they often faced racial taunts from fans and other players. I do not believe this represents equal access. I think the term *desegregation* more accurately conveys the fact that the process happened slowly over a long time. Signing one player of color to a team did not resolve the racial issues related to that team. The signing of the player began the process that required other players, changing access to restaurants and hotels, and evolving views of players, management, and fans. Since players of color continued to face racism and discrimination after they joined a team, the addition of a player of color on a team did not end the discrimination. The players still roomed alone or with other players of color. They still faced challenges in securing hotel rooms or meals. While I think *desegregation* better reflects this ongoing and complicated process, I will use *integration* because it is the common language of the study of this process.

ORGANIZATION

The overall structure of the book includes five chapters that tell the story of the integration of the Pacific Coast League from 1907 to 1952. It focuses on the period of 1948–52, when thirty-one players integrated PCL teams. Since the story of the players who had integrated the PCL teams has never been told, I tried to include the basic information for each player on each team in chronological order throughout the chapters. The order was the San Diego Padres (1948), the Oakland Oaks (1949), the Portland Beavers (1949), the Los Angeles Angels (1949), the Sacramento Solons (1950), the San Francisco Seals (1951), the Hollywood Stars (1951), and the Seattle Rainiers (1952).

Chapter 1 examines the color line and the PCL before World War II. While the PCL excluded black players, it allowed Native Americans, Native Hawaiians, and Asian Americans on team rosters. African Americans, or those players who were perceived to be black, found a color line that they could not cross. The practice of segregation was based not on nonwhite but on whether others defined a player as black. While some may argue that players such as Lang Akana and Jimmy Claxton integrated the Pacific Coast League, they were individual exceptions to a larger practice that was not changed until after World War II.

Challenges to segregation in the PCL from a variety of sources, including players, the black press, and local communities, are discussed in chapter 2. The pressure kept the issue of integration in the public view. That pressure began to yield cracks, and a handful of players received tryouts or promises of tryouts during World War II. Just a few months after the end of the war, Branch Rickey signed Jackie Robinson. With his first season in the International League as a Montreal Royal, Robinson integrated the Minor Leagues first. As other Minor Leagues integrated in 1946 and 1947, the door was opened for the integration of the PCL in 1948.

The focus of chapter 3 is John Ritchey and his role in integrating the San Diego Padres and the Pacific Coast League in 1948. Ritchey, a native of San Diego, grew up in a California defined by racial rules that were fluid and flexible. While his family lived in a segregated community, he attended an integrated high school and played on integrated baseball teams. When the San Diego Padres added Ritchey to their roster, the team joined a social movement already under way in other baseball leagues.

By 1949, as described in chapter 4, integration had moved beyond the San Diego Padres to three other PCL teams. By my definition of integration, this is when integration becomes a movement for social change and civil rights. It is no longer connected to just one individual. The players who integrated teams in 1949 not only increased in number but also included dark-skinned Latinos as well as African Americans. The players continued to face racism, but the process of integration had now spread beyond one player and one team.

In chapter 5 I describe the integration of the remaining four PCL teams, which integrated between 1950 and 1952. The pace of integration across all levels of professional baseball and within the PCL increased rapidly and moved more quickly than at the Major League level. As the PCL teams each signed a player or players of color, more followed. Some Major League teams refused to recognize the inevitability of integration, and one Minor League, the Southern Association, ended rather than integrating. The signing of player of color after player of color to team after team year after year represents a forward momentum that would not be stopped. True integration began not in 1916 but in 1948.

In a short afterword, I note what happened to each of the players who integrated a team of the Pacific Coast League.

CHAPTER 1

BASEBALL, THE COLOR LINE, AND THE PACIFIC COAST LEAGUE BEFORE WORLD WAR II

I had been with Oakland about a month when I got notice I was released.
No reason was given, but I knew.
Jimmy Claxton, interview, 1964

He held many jobs during his lifetime: elevator operator, laborer, longshore-man, stevedore, asphalt raker, janitor, and coal miner. He was also a baseball player. He played baseball for many years, mostly in small towns across the Pacific Northwest and in California. He pitched for barnstorming teams, all-black teams, and company teams. For one day in May 1916, he pitched two and one-third innings for another team, the Oakland Oaks of the Pacific Coast League. Records label James Edgar Claxton a man of mixed parent-age, both black and white, during his lifetime. Not all in Oakland welcomed the lineage that Jimmy Claxton traced through his father back to Africa, and manager Rowdy Elliott released Claxton from the team. Claxton later recalled that it was because of his race. While some would mark Claxton as the first African American in the Pacific Coast League, he did not integrate the league. Called a Native American by the Oaks for convenience and playing for the team for only one day, Claxton is a noteworthy figure, but not one who changed society. That change would not come to the Pacific Coast League for another thirty-two years.

On March 30, 1948, a young African American catcher joined the roster of the San Diego Padres. Born and raised in San Diego, John Ritchey became the first African American to join a Pacific Coast League team. He would not be the last. The process of integrating the eight teams of the PCL took five seasons. The PCL was not the first Minor League to integrate, but it was the first Minor or Major League to integrate all of its teams. As an organization professional baseball segregated in the late nineteenth century. Individual players and teams would challenge that color line. Efforts to sign players of color began in the early 1900s when two different team PCL teams, the Portland Beavers and the Oakland Oaks, attempted to change the practice of segregation in the PCL by signing nonwhite players. Players of color, including Native Hawaiians, Asians, and Asian Americans, who played, or attempted to play, in the Pacific Coast League before 1948 were excluded because, for the PCL, the definition of nonwhite seemed to center on whether the player appeared to be black.

Founded just after the turn of the twentieth century, the Pacific Coast League traced its roots to the nineteenth century. Baseball came to California with the gold rush of 1849. The first team organized in San Francisco in 1859. After the Civil War a variety of leagues came and went throughout California and the Pacific Coast. In 1903 teams from California joined with teams from the Pacific Northwest to create the Pacific Coast League. The original teams were in Los Angeles, San Francisco, Oakland, Sacramento, Portland, and Seattle. The league continued, with some variation in teams and locations, through the 1957 season, the year before two Major League teams, the Brooklyn Dodgers and New York Giants, moved to California, supplanting the popular Minor League teams.

The Pacific Coast League continued a tradition of professional baseball begun in the East during the nineteenth century. By the beginning of the twentieth century, the National and American Leagues agreed to a governing body. The National League had formed in 1876. After its founding in 1901 the American League challenged the National League for control of professional baseball. In 1903 the two leagues signed the National Agreement for the Government of Baseball Clubs, also called the National Agreement. It was an agreement that resolved their conflicting business interests and formed complementary practices.[1] The National Agreement set out territorial rights, recognized the contracts of each league with its players, and established a three-member commission that would settle disagreements between the leagues, impose fines, and arrange for the best team from each league to play against one another in the World Series, which began in 1903.[2] The National Agreement also formally established the hierarchy of Major and Minor Leagues that placed the Major League teams as the better skilled and better paid. In 1902 the various Minor Leagues had formed their own organization, the National Association of Professional Base Ball Players, or National Association. In the first year fourteen different Minor Leagues participated in the agreement that established a hierarchical structure of classifications within the Minors based on playing ability. Through the twentieth century the rankings included, from highest to lowest, Triple-A, Double-A, A, and, at times, B, C, D, and Rookie levels. In 1903 the signing of the National Agreement established an overarching umbrella structure that would govern all of professional baseball, but the Major and Minor League teams would conduct business separately. Major and Minor League teams may have been part of the same professional sport, governed by the same rules, but each team had its own management that oversaw the business of its team. Other teams or leagues also existed, but unless they participated in the National Agreement, professional baseball labeled them as independent and not part of their organization or administrative structure. *Organized baseball* is a term used by baseball historians to describe the Major and Minor Leagues. Amateur leagues, independent leagues, and the Negro Leagues are not included in this definition.

The Pacific Coast League was one of three leagues at the top of the Minor League hierarchy. It had its own league management, including a Board of Directors composed of a president and the owners of each team. The PCL season lasted longer than other leagues, sometimes up to two hundred games a season. After 1930, when night baseball was introduced, in most years clubs played a six-day series from Tuesday to Sunday with a day game on Saturday and a doubleheader on Sunday.[3]

A more direct connection between the business operations of the Major and Minor League teams began in the 1920s, when Branch Rickey, then both president and general manager of the St. Louis Cardinals, created a new idea for Major League teams, a farm system. By contracting with Minor League teams, a Major League team could develop their future players. The Major League teams owned the contracts of the players rather than the Minor League team. The management of the Major League team made decisions about the placement of that player within its system of teams, from the Major League team down through the various skill levels of the Minor League teams, selecting a level of play that best suited the player and the Major League team. Minor League teams owned their stadia and hired their own management but did not have a say in the decisions related to player contracts. Today, almost all Minor League teams have a Major League team affiliation, which gives the Major League team control of the contracts of each player.[4] These affiliations cross national boundaries and include teams in Canada and Mexico.

In the 1940s leagues across Latin America found many players from the United States joining their teams. Established as an amateur league, the Mexican League expanded and professionalized in the 1930s. During this period players from the United States began to leave their contracts and "jumped" to teams in Mexico. Mexican teams offered players more money and, for African Americans, greater acceptance in society.[5] Satchel Paige, the famous Negro League pitcher, was the first African American player to head south in 1938. In 1940 the Mexican League divided into two six-team leagues, and owners actively recruited players from the United States to fill their rosters. After World War II, as the Mexican Leagues increased their recruitment of white players from the United States, the Mexican League rosters became a mixture of black, white, and Latino players from both sides of the border. In 1946 owner Jorge Pasquel offered better-paying contracts to players from the Major Leagues as well as the Negro Leagues. Major League Baseball commissioner A. B. "Happy" Chandler instituted a five-year suspension for any player who abandoned his contract to play in a foreign league.[6] The practice quickly ended.

In the off-season winter months many professional baseball players traveled to the Caribbean or South America to play baseball in warm-weather climates. Leagues formed in Puerto Rico, the Dominican Republic, as well as Cuba and Venezuela.[7] The ability to play in Latin America offered black players the opportunity to improve their baseball skills as well as to experience life outside of the segregated United States.

In the second half of the nineteenth century, as the system of Jim Crow developed across the South, racism also found its way onto the baseball diamond. In the decades after the Civil War, black players such as Moses Fleetwood Walker and Bud Flower played on integrated teams until a color line, first attempted in the 1860s and formalized across professional baseball by the 1880s, prevented blacks from playing on teams with whites.[8] All-black teams formed to allow black players to continue playing baseball. Segregation in baseball challenged the basic notion of fielding the best team to win the game. Owners supporting segregation decided to overlook superior players who were African American, or who appeared to be African American, and instead enforced society's color line that excluded them.

The first attempt at segregation in baseball began just after the Civil War, in 1867, at the organizational level. The National Association of Base Ball Players passed a resolution refusing admission to the league any team with "one or more colored persons."[9] The provision ended when the organization did in 1871.

On July 14, 1887, the board of the International League, a Minor League trying to compete with the National League, approved a ban on contracts with black players. During the same period some white players began to refuse to participate with black players, including Adrian "Cap" Anson. In 1883 Anson challenged the inclusion of Fleetwood Walker, a black player, on the lineup of the opposing team, but did not succeed in getting Walker removed.[10] Just four years later in 1887, with the International League, a Minor League in the East, now accepting a color line, Anson, the manager and star player of the Chicago White Stockings, threatened to refuse to field his team against a team with a black player. This time he succeeded, thus marking the first time a manager openly supported segregation.[11] The refusal of any team to sign an African American began a period of collusion by the owners in support of segregation.

African Americans formed their own teams and leagues, with the greatest success coming in 1920 when Rube Foster founded the Negro National League. The National Agreement of 1903 and the organizational structure of baseball did not include Negro League teams, which professional baseball considered outside of their purview. Segregation, already established across professional baseball, became part of the Pacific Coast League from its founding.

During the period of segregation in professional baseball, teams attempted to circumvent the practice of segregation by adding Native Americans to their rosters, although some of the players were Native Americans in name only. Between 1897 and 1945 Major League Baseball included forty-five Native American players and eighty-five players with some Native American ancestry and hundreds more in Minor League Baseball.[12] Professional baseball and fans judged these players using stereotypes and called them "Chief." In 1897 Louis Sockalexis, a member of the Penobscot tribe in Maine, joined the Cleveland Spiders. Historians note that although he played in only ninety-four games during three seasons at the Major League level before alcoholism took over his life, Louis Sockalexis was the first Native American to play in professional baseball.[13] In 1901 Baltimore Oriole manager John McGraw renamed African American Charlie Grant as Chief Tokahoma and presented him as a Cherokee Indian. Others discovered the false portrayal when the team traveled to Chicago, a place in which Charlie Grant had played previously with the Columbia Giants, a professional black team.[14]

The 1910s saw three well-known players of Native American ancestry: Charles "Chief" Bender, John "Chief" Meyers, and Jim Thorpe. Born in Minnesota, Charles Bender attended the Carlisle Indian Industrial School in Carlisle, Pennsylvania. Bender pitched for the Philadelphia Athletics from 1903 to 1917. In 1910 in an interview with the *Chicago Daily News*, Bender said he had not faced discrimination and had "been treated the same as other men," but he remembered hearing war whoops from the crowds.[15] Catcher John Meyers, born in Riverside, California, had a nine-year career in the Majors, including seven seasons with the New York Giants from 1909 to 1915. Later in life during several interviews, he remembered the struggles with race as a player: "And I don't like to say this, but in those days, when I was young, I was considered a foreigner. I didn't belong. I was an Indian."[16] Although accepted to a certain point, Native people still faced discrimination by whites. After a successful football career at the Carlisle Indian Industrial School, the Oklahoma-born Thorpe, of the Fox and Sac tribes, won gold medals at the 1912 Olympics in Sweden for the decathlon and pentathlon. In 1913 the Amateur Athletic Union revoked Thorpe's amateur status after a newspaper reported that Thorpe earned money playing on semipro baseball teams.[17] Jim Thorpe joined the New York Giants in 1913, the beginning of a six-year Major League Baseball career.[18]

None of the previously mentioned players had Native American ancestry from both parents. In 1921 the Pittsburgh Pirates signed Moses YellowHorse, a full-blooded Pawnee.[19] YellowHorse pitched in thirty-eight games for the Pirates over two seasons. In 1922 the Pirates traded YellowHorse to the Sacramento Senators of the PCL, with whom he played for two seasons. His professional baseball career ended in 1936 with the Omaha Robin Hoods. Through the 1920s and 1930s other players of Native American ancestry played in the Majors, but without as much success. The Baseball Hall of Fame Veterans Committee elected two Native Americans to its hallowed halls, Charles Bender in 1953 and Zack Wheat in 1959. These players lived during a time when whites accepted the assimilation of Native Americans, but in a limited way. They may have had some Native ancestry, but each would still experience differing levels of acceptance throughout professional baseball.

In the Pacific Coast League attempts to sign players in Portland and Oakland in the 1900s and 1910s demonstrate that blackness defined the line of segregation in baseball. The issue for those who supported segregation was not that the player was nonwhite; the issue was whether others perceived the player to be black. Two Hawaiian players identified as having dark skin played in the PCL. In the 1910s the custom of skin-colored segregation restricted two players, whom other people identified as black, from playing. While these owners and managers did not express a desire to reinforce or change the system, Barney Joy, John Williams, Lang Akana, and Jimmy Claxton are players whose experience demonstrates the color line was about blackness.

During a barnstorming trip to Hawaii in the winter of 1914–15, Portland Beaver owner Walter McCredie signed Lang Akana, a player with native Hawaiian and Chinese ancestry. Akana was not the first but the third player with Native Hawaiian ancestry signed by a Pacific Coast League team. The first, Barney Joy, a half-Chinese and half-Hawaiian pitcher, played in forty-nine games for the San Francisco Seals in 1907. On March 8, 1907, an article in the *San Francisco Chronicle* described Joy as "dark, but not so dark as the average native Hawaiian."[20] Described by the *San Francisco Chronicle* throughout the season as Hawaiian, Joy appeared to be accepted by the team and the Pacific Coast League.[21] The *San Francisco Examiner* described Barney Joy as a "husky brown-skinned lad."[22] Although they were highlighting his skin color, they did not label Joy as black. The distinction between black and brown skin would allow Barney Joy to play for the Seals.

A second Native Hawaiian pitcher, John B. "Honolulu Johnnie" Williams threw for the Sacramento Sacts in 1911. With one-quarter Hawaiian ancestry coming from his maternal grandmother, Williams would be the first Hawaiian to play in the Major Leagues. Although the majority of his six seasons in professional baseball would be spent in the Minors, Williams pitched in four games in the Major Leagues with the Detroit Tigers in 1914. The *Sacramento Bee* called him "Dusky" Williams.[23] As with Barney Joy, the newspaper noted the color of Williams's skin color. Later, Williams would become "Honolulu Johnnie." With Williams's acceptance into the Major Leagues, reference to his skin color becomes a geographical one. By including "Hawaiian," this moniker explains why his skin color was not white while also clarifying that he was not black, and thus could cross the color line. Although these players were sometimes darker skinned, the Native Hawaiian categorization allowed them to play in organized baseball. That categorization would not be true for Lang Akana.

On December 27, 1914, a headline in the *Los Angeles Times* read, "McCredie Is Forced to Fire Chinese Because White Men Balk: No Chink Will Play Baseball." This headline captured the world of Walter McCredie, one that did not allow nonwhites to play professional baseball and one that accepted the use of racist terms like *chink*. Iowa-born Portland Beavers owner Walter McCredie faced friction from his team when he signed Lang Akana, a half-Hawaiian and half-Chinese player, after an all-star trip to Hawaii. Despite having the same family heritage as Barney Joy, Lang Akana was seen by others as black. McCredie said, "His skin is too dark. . . . I have received a couple of letters from players telling me Akana is as dark as Jack Johnson, so I guess I will have to give him a release." McCredie's response about the release also included a statement of support for nonwhite players because, he argued, the Major leagues already included Native American and Cuban players:

> I don't think the color of the skin ought to be a barrier in baseball. . . . They have Jim Thorpe, an Indian, in the big leagues; there are Cubans on the

rosters of the various clubs. Here in the Pacific Coast League we have a Mexican and a Hawaiian, and yet the laws of baseball bar Afro-Americans from organized diamonds. If I had my say the Afro-Americans would be welcome inside the fold. I would like to have two such ball players as [Bruce] Petway and [John Henry "Pop"] Lloyd of the Chicago Colored Giants, who play out here every spring [in the California Winter League].

Walter McCredie, aware of the diversity of quality ball players, was a manager willing to evaluate a player based on skill rather than skin color. Earlier in the year, in March 1914, McCredie spoke out against PCL president Allen T. Baum's decision to prevent Rube Foster's Chicago American Giants, a Negro League team playing in the California Winter League, from using Pacific Coast League ballparks on their barnstorming tour through the West. Cal Ewing, owner of the San Francisco Seals and the Oakland Oaks, supported Baum's decision, but McCredie did not. He invited the Chicago American Giants to Portland to play against the Beavers. The Giants won four of the five games. McCredie wanted to make it a yearly event.[24]

McCredie's statements about Lang Akana highlight three issues related to the PCL and the definition of the color line. First, the Minor League structure supported a policy of segregation, while some individuals, like McCredie, did not. Second, in 1915, in the weeks before the film *Birth of a Nation* debuted in Los Angeles, McCredie publicly stated he would like to hire a nonwhite player. He would like to have hired players based on their skill, but was restricted by some players on his team and by the league. Finally, while there were individuals like McCredie who worked to change the accepted customs, there was not enough support across the league for racial integration. The league and American society supported the continued practice of discriminating against blackness.

In the West African American players regularly played against white players. The California Winter League, which began about 1910, allowed teams of white players to play against teams of black players.[25] That league permitted blacks to play exhibition games against an all-white team, but in 1914 the Pacific Coast League would not. While the California Winter League was not an integrated league because players of color did not compete on the same teams as whites, it was an important step toward integration by providing a venue to display the skills of blacks playing against whites and winning. California offered several such examples of blacks and whites playing against one another during the years of baseball's segregation.

McCredie's statements also show that issues of race in America went beyond a simple black-white binary. The racial dynamic in the country, but particularly on the West Coast, included racial diversity. By looking beyond black and white, McCredie recognized that Native American, Hispanic, and Asian players were available to sign. McCredie had to release Lang Akana the year before the signing of the multiracial Jimmy Claxton by the Oakland Oaks.

In 1916 the signing of an African American player to the Oakland Oaks demonstrates both the criteria that defined the line of segregation and the attempt to circumvent it. In May 1916 Jimmy Claxton played in two games for the Oakland Oaks. Claxton's appearance in these two games causes some to consider Claxton to be the player who "integrated" the PCL. James Edgar Claxton was born on December 14, 1892, in the coal-mining town of Wellington,[26] on Vancouver Island in British Columbia, Canada, to American parents. Jimmy Claxton's father, William Edgar, a black Lynchburg, Virginia, farmer, was a widower when he met and married Jimmy's mother, Emma Richards, a white woman born in Illinois, the daughter of a farmer. She had moved with her family to Washington State as a teenager.[27] Claxton's family background included black, French, Indian, Irish, and English ancestors. Documents recording the family lineage illustrate the variety of designations for mixed-race families in the United States. In the 1870 U.S. Census from Lynchburg, the census taker lists Claxton's paternal grandfather as mulatto and his paternal grandmother as black. William Claxton next appears in the 1891 Census of Canada as living as a lodger in Wellington with other Americans, but race is not a category of inquiry in the Canadian Census.[28] Less than a year later, on January 14, 1892, William Claxton and Emma Richards married. On the marriage certificate the reverend who married them noted, "The bridegroom is a coloured man; the bride a white woman."[29] The Claxtons had three children: James Edgar, born December 14, 1892, in Wellington; John Frederick, born November 15, 1894, in Tacoma; and Emma Elmary Josephin, born August 16, 1896, in Wellington.[30] Different federal documents would note each of the three children as white, mulatto, and black. These documents show the Claxton family to be not only a mixed-race family but also one whose racial classification changed over time, depending on what other races the government found them to be living with.

As a child Jimmy Claxton would not have been the one to define his race for the census taker. When Jimmy Claxton's race designation changed again in 1900, the census taker shows that other people defined the race of the Claxton children. In 1900 the Claxton children lived in Tacoma, Washington, but not with either of their parents. The 1900 U.S. Census listed Jimmy as James Clarkston, and he lived with Charlie and Mary Steel. The Steels lived next door to Claxton's maternal grandparents, Michael and Myra Richards. A note in the column for "year of immigration to the United States" included the remark "1898, guardians did not know." On the same page, the census lists John and Emma as living with their maternal relatives, two doors away from their maternal grandparents. A note in the margin says, "Myra Richards is the guardian for these three children."[31] For all three children the census taker listed their race as white. When they were living with white relatives in 1900, the Claxton children received the designation of white. The changing designation of Jimmy Claxton's race was an example of the flexibility of race in the West in general and for those with a mixed heritage more specifically.

A decade later the racial designation of the Claxton children changed, this time dividing the siblings between two races. In the 1910 census Emma lived with her maternal grandparents in Spokane, Washington, with her race listed again as white. William, now listed as divorced, and James and John were boarders in a house in Ravensdale, Washington. The census taker listed the race of all three as mulatto. William and James were coal miners. In the same census Emma Claxton, with "widowed" listed as her marital status, worked as a chambermaid for a hotel in Tacoma. The 1910 census listed Claxton's race as mulatto. His sister, raised by maternal grandparents, received the designation of white. On his World War I draft registration card, Jimmy Claxton's race is "Ethiopian." The 1920 census listed William, James, and John all with the racial designation of black. That same year the census recorded Emma as the wife of Ernest C. Tanner, a black longshoreman. Given her marriage to a black man, Emma's racial designation changed from white to mulatto.[32] This history of changing racial designation of the Claxton family shows that Claxton did not easily fit into one category. Those with whom Jimmy Claxton associated changed his racial designation. Had Jimmy Claxton found a way to continue to record his race as white, his baseball career might have included more than two games in organized baseball.

In the spring of 1916 Jimmy Claxton pitched for the all-black Oak Leafs, engaging in social subterfuge. A Native American fan of the team introduced Claxton as a "fellow tribesman" to the Oakland Oaks secretary. The Oaks signed Claxton and introduced him as Native American.[33] The *San Francisco Chronicle* noted, "Claxton, the Indian pitcher who works from the port side and hails from an Indian reservation in Minnesota, is to do the honors for the Oaks this morning. . . . There is more or less curiosity to see what Claxton has to offer, for it will be his Coast League debut."[34] Claxton was on the Oakland Oaks' roster for a week, but he pitched in only two games before the team released him from his contract. On Sunday, May 28, 1916, Claxton pitched in both games of a doubleheader against the Los Angeles Angels, finishing the first and starting the second, for a combined two and one-third innings. He pitched two innings of the first game and allowed three runs, four hits, and three walks, leaving the game with the Oaks behind by a score of 0–3. He then pitched to the leadoff batter in the second game, walking him.[35] An interesting side note to the historic moment was the report that a riot broke out in the ninth inning of the first game. The riot, which appeared to be unrelated to Claxton as he was not in the game at the time and pitched in the second game, began over the belief by the Oaks that a runner should have been called out.[36]

Within the week the Oaks released Jimmy Claxton. Whether his dismissal was because of his poor performance or his race, Claxton believed it to be the latter. In an interview with the *Contra Costa Times* in 1964, Claxton said the team did not give a reason for his release, but he knew it was because of his color. "No reason was given, but I knew." Claxton told his son that fans who witnessed Claxton kiss his black wife in the stands went to the team's management to complain, and this was the reason for his accelerated release.[37] The Oakland Oaks' manager, Harold "Rowdy" Elliott, said Claxton did not have the skills for the PCL.[38]

Claxton had played locally for black teams, and it seems difficult to believe that the Oaks' management knew nothing about his racial background before signing him. The *Oakland Tribune* printed several articles between February and May that reported Claxton as a member of the Oak Leafs, a team of blacks, even including an image of the pitcher. On May 15, 1916, the *Tribune* reported that the manager, Elliott, was expecting two new players, Jimmy Claxton and Ed Klein. There is no mention of Claxton's race in the articles. The next day the paper reported that Claxton was not to have the opportunity for a trial. The next week the Oakland Oaks publicized the addition of Jimmy Claxton to the team. The *San Francisco Chronicle* noted, "Elliott is decidedly optimistic over George [sic] Claxton, Indian southpaw, who has been with the team for a couple of weeks. Claxton comes from one of the Indian reservations in the Middle West with a good record of games won. He pitched to the batters yesterday, and chances are that very shortly he will be given a chance in the box."[39]

On May 25, 1916, the *Oakland Tribune* reported, "Pitcher Klaxton [sic], a full-blooded Indian, who has been making a great record in semi-pro baseball in these parts lately, has been signed by Rowdy Elliott, and will probably be given a try in the box some time this week. Klaxton is well known, both in Portland and around the bay cities, where he has made an enviable record in semi-pro circles. His first pitching was done in Minneapolis, where he went from the Minnesota reservation."

As the Oakland Oaks could not deny the previous stories about the teams on which Claxton played, they attempted to alter his race from African American to Native American to fit the acceptable standards of the time. Their attempts to present him as Native American fitted into the structure of segregation in professional baseball when the sport excluded African Americans but welcomed Native Americans.

In a twist of history the Collins-McCarthy Candy Company, which produced the "Zeenut" trading cards, happened to take photos of the team the week Claxton appeared on the roster. His card, the first to include an African American, was card 25 in a series of 143. After his brief tenure with the Oaks, Claxton never played in professional baseball again. Jimmy Claxton died March 3, 1970, in Tacoma, Washington, and his family buried him at the Oakwood Hill Cemetery in Tacoma. Thus, Jimmy Claxton became a notable figure in the history of segregation in the Pacific Coast League, but not the person who would be the first of many creating a movement for social change.

From the 1900s to the 1940s, even as state and federal laws restricted their lives, Asian Americans demonstrated pride in their local communities as well as a connection to American culture through baseball. Professional baseball did not restrict Asian and Asian American players in the same way as African American players, but they had a limited presence in the Pacific Coast League. The most notable players from the pre–World War II era were a Chinese American and a Japanese American who pitched against one another in the PCL in 1932.

Baseball teams and leagues existed from Southern California to Washington State. In 1903 San Francisco saw the founding of the Fuji Athletic Club.[40] In Seattle an all-Issei league formed by 1910.[41] At a game that year five hundred fans watched the Seattle Mikados defeat the Tacoma Columbias for the Issei Pacific Northwest Championship.[42] In the 1910s the Hawaiian Travelers made several barnstorming trips to the mainland.[43] A team from the Chinese Athletic Club played in San Francisco in 1918.[44] Two years later Mas Akizuki founded the Asahi Baseball Club in San Jose.[45] A colony of Japanese farmers also formed teams in Livingston, California. In the Central Valley Japanese League (1934–41), local churches and merchants sponsored eight teams.[46] The Oakland Wah Sung baseball team won many games across the Bay Area in the 1930s.[47] In Portland, Oregon, Kats Nakayama founded the Nippon Giants, a baseball team of local Nisei.[48] In Los Angeles Issei and Nisei played on the Los Angeles Nippons Baseball Club between 1926 and 1941. They played against other teams of Japanese Americans, sometimes at the Los Angeles Angels' Wrigley Field.[49] In Seattle the *Japanese-American Courier* sponsored a baseball league from 1928 to 1941 as part of its promotion of recreation for the Japanese American community.[50] During World War II Japanese Americans played softball and baseball during their forced internment.[51]

Between 1929 and 1936, in addition to Native Hawaiian players, four PCL teams included Asian American players. PCL teams accepted two Native Hawaiian players in the 1900s and 1910s and continued to do so in the 1920s and 1930s. The Native Hawaiian–Portuguese Henry Oana played for the San Francisco Seals from 1929 to 1932 and the Portland Beavers in 1933 and 1934. Oana would be the first Native Hawaiian to play in the Major Leagues when he joined the Philadelphia Phillies in 1934. Native Hawaiian and Chinese like Barney Joy, John M. "Johnny" Kerr played one game with the San Francisco Seals in 1936. Native Hawaiian Clarence Kumalae had a tryout with the Los Angeles Angels in 1933, and although he did not make a PCL team roster, he did join the semiprofessional Catalina Cubs.[52] The only possible negative reference in the *Los Angeles Times* about the place of origin of any of the three players came on May 9, 1933, after the San Francisco Seals traded Henry Oana to the Portland Beavers. "Oana has been hitting the pineapple with much gusto since joining the Ducks [Beavers] and latest reports are that the Seal owners have chewed their fingernails down to the quick."[53]

In the 1920s three Asian Americans joined the Native Hawaiian players in the PCL. Fumito "Jimmy" Horio, a Japanese American born in Hawaii, played twenty games with the Sacramento Senators in 1935. The *Los Angeles Times* noted that Horio was the "only Japanese player in organized baseball." Author Bob Ray described Horio as Japanese when in fact he was a Hawaiian-born Japanese American. The *Los Angeles Times* would use the descriptor *Japanese* many times during coverage of the 1935 season, including for "Jimmy Horio Day" when Horio was "honored by his countrymen," although that report also noted that he was born in Hawaii. Both the San Francisco Seals and the Los Angeles Angels held a Jimmy Horio Day for the Sacramento Solon, on August 25 and September 1, respectively.[54] The teams seemed pleased to be able to bring Japanese and Japanese American fans to the ballpark. The most notable moment for Asian Americans in the PCL happened in 1932, when two Asian Americans, Japanese American Kenso Nushida and Chinese American Lee Gum Hong, pitched against one another in another attempt by PCL teams to increase ticket sales.

In the summer of 1932 the Sacramento Senators signed Japanese American Kenso Nushida. Born in Hawaii, the five-foot-one, 109-pound left-handed pitcher lived in Stockton.[55] Nushida had pitched for teams in Hawaii, on Japanese American teams in the Central Valley, and on three all-star Japanese teams from America who toured Japan.[56] He pitched fifty-eight innings in eleven games for the Solons, from August 10 to the end of the season. Sacramento Senators owner Lew Moreing estimated that attendance doubled on the days that Nushida pitched.[57] More than just a gate attraction, Kenso Nushida was also a quality pitcher.[58] As Nushida brought in larger crowds in each city the Solons played, the Oakland Oaks thought they might also benefit from signing an Asian American player. While fighting to stay out of last place for the 1932 season, the Oakland Oaks signed Lee Gum Hong, also known as Albert Bowen, a pitcher on the Wah Sung team, a Chinese American baseball team. The teams hoped that the presence of two Asian American players would bring more fans into the stands.[59] The Oaks announced that twenty-year-old Lee Gum Hong, an Oakland High School graduate and employee at the International House near the University of California at Berkeley, would pitch in the last series of the season. The opening game of the series, on Wednesday, September 28, 1932, would see Hong pitch against Kenso Nushida and the Solons.[60] This would be not only the first game featuring two opposing Asian American pitchers, but also a battle parallel to the ongoing international tensions between China and Japan. The pitchers played two games against one another in the last week of the season. The first game had three thousand fans watching in Oak Park in Emeryville. Nushida pitched for four and one-third innings before leaving the game. Four days later in the last game of the season, Lee and the Oaks beat Nushida and the Solons in the second game of the Sunday double-header.[61] Neither of the players returned to their PCL team, nor did either play in professional baseball again, although the Solons offered Nushida subsequent contracts.[62] Although not in large numbers, Asian Americans were included on PCL rosters during integration. The participation of Asian Americans in the PCL shows that segregation was not defined by nonwhite; it was defined by whether the player was perceived to be black.

The color line in the Pacific Coast League clearly focused on segregating those who were defined by others as black, even if they did not define themselves that way. With the signing of Lang Akana and Jimmy Claxton, the managers attempted to blur the color line, but they did not succeed. The social standards at the time, including those in the West, centered on if the athlete appeared to have African ancestry. While some players of color, like Native Hawaiians and Asian Americans, could play on PCL teams, if the public perceived an individual to have darker skin, the team would reject him. The color line held firm. The challenges to the system of segregation began to increase during the 1940s and would finally break in 1948.

CHAPTER 2

BASEBALL, THE COLOR LINE, AND THE PACIFIC COAST LEAGUE IN THE 1940S

My brother said one team was very interested in signing him. This may have been the White Sox or one of the PCL teams. I'm not sure. But this team wanted him to "pass" as an Indian. My mother's mother was Cherokee and my father also had Indian blood, so Nate probably has more Indian blood than Negro blood. But Nate didn't want any part of "passing." That would be like getting into baseball by the back door. He always walked tall. It wasn't about race, it was about accepting him as he was.
Toni Stewart, brother of Nate Moreland, quoted in John Reynolds, "Nate Moreland: A Mystery to Historians"

Nate Moreland's life paralleled Jackie Robinson's. Born in different southern states, both men moved with their families to Southern California in 1920. After graduating from Muir Tech High School in Pasadena, their paths parted ways. Jackie Robinson attended Pasadena Community College, and Nate Moreland matriculated at Redlands University. After playing semipro baseball for a year, Robinson and Moreland petitioned the Chicago White Sox for tryouts during their spring training in Pasadena in March 1942. Two PCL teams offered Nate Moreland tryouts in 1943. After completing their military service in World War II, and playing briefly in the Negro Leagues, the men would each integrate a league. Jackie Robinson integrated the Montreal Royals of the International League and Nate Moreland the El Centro Imperials of the Sunset League. While Robinson would move up to the Brooklyn Dodgers in 1947, Moreland would never make it to the big leagues. This generation of baseball players experienced both segregation and integration. The shift to integrated teams happened not because those in charge changed their minds about the gentlemen's agreement, but because of the activism of individuals who wanted to see baseball integrate. While individuals such as Lang Akana and Jimmy Claxton were attempts to challenge the status quo, it would not be until World War II that individuals would join together to move the PCL toward integration. In the 1940s individual players, the black and white press in the West, community organizations, and fans pressured the Major and Minor Leagues to bend and ultimately break the color line in professional baseball.

During the 1930s and 1940s West Coast newspaper journalists voiced their support for the end of segregating sports. In California white reporter Art Cohn and three African American Los Angeles–area journalists, Edward "Abie" Robinson (*Los Angeles Sentinel, San Francisco Sun-Reporter*), William Claire "Halley" Harding (*Los Angeles Tribune*), and Herman Hill (West Coast Bureau chief of the *Pittsburgh Courier*), played an important role in advocating or promoting integration. In Northern California readers of the *Oakland Tribune* read columns by Art Cohn about the integration of sport. During his journalism career Cohn brought to the attention of his readers many racial injustices. In 1936 he posted an open letter to U.S. Olympic Committee chair Avery Brundage, protesting the participation of the U.S. Olympic team in the Berlin Games. "You and your bootlickers forced the United States to send an Olympic team to Nazi Germany in 1936 when every decent-thinking American was dead set against it. That was no sport festival, it was a political demonstration. You, as America's representative, made no outcry when the Nazis insulted Jesse Owens. Hell, you didn't even bat an eyelash when a couple of Jewish boys couldn't make the trip to Berlin because they might affront Herr Hitler. No, Avery, you have never stood up for the so-called principles for which the Olympic Games are supposed to stand." He also protested discrimination in football: "Fourteen East-West games have been played. But no Negro, no matter how outstanding, has ever played in them. It is an unwritten law, immutable as the commandment that bars Negroes from organized baseball."[1]

As a white sports reporter, Art Cohn saw and wrote about discrimination during World War II. In 1943, as a writer for the *Oakland Tribune*, Cohn asked if Senator Sheridan Downey of California could propose a congressional investigation of discrimination against Negroes in the war effort, wondering why there could not be a similar probe of discrimination against blacks in baseball.[2] Cohn worked as a sports correspondent for the *Long Beach Independent* from July 1 to November 1945. His time at the *Independent* was so limited because he opposed the move of high school football from day to night games. At the end of the annual Poly-Wilson game, students, "outraged by his effort, burned him in effigy . . . bombarded him with anti-Semitic epithets and tomatoes."[3] Cohn's editor would not allow him to respond in his column, so he quit and became a writer for Hollywood. Shortly before his death Cohn returned to journalism as a feature columnist for the *San Francisco Examiner*.[4] After his death on March 22, 1958, newspaper articles remembered Art Cohn, a passenger in a twin-engine plane that crashed in the Zuni Mountains near Grants, New Mexico, as a screenwriter rather than a sports reporter who championed racial equality.[5]

Among the first African American reporters making a more concerted effort to force the integration of society and sport was Edward "Abie" Robinson. Born in 1916 in New Orleans, Robinson moved to Los Angeles with his family in 1920. Robinson's employment in journalism began at the black-owned *Los Angeles Sentinel*. His responsibilities also included "sports editor, assistant circulation and advertising managers and public relations liaison." Robinson worked at the *California Eagle* from 1951 to 1964. As a reporter for the *Los Angeles Sentinel*, Abie Robinson organized community participation in the paper's successful 1934 campaign "Don't Spend Your Money Where You Can't Work." The protests included pickets and boycotts of white-owned stores on Central Avenue that would not hire black employees.[6] In the late 1930s Robinson organized a picket of a local theater showing the film *Tales of Manhattan*. The protest against racial stereotypes in the film led to the founding of the Beverly Hills–Hollywood branch of the National Association for the

Advancement of Colored People. His social activism included advocating for the hiring of black musicians in the Academy Awards band as well as the hiring of black teachers by the Los Angeles Unified School District in 1954.[7]

Abie Robinson wrote a regular column for the *Los Angeles Sentinel* called "Abie's Corner." In one such column on May 30, 1946, Robinson thanked Bill Sweeney, manager of the Los Angeles Angels, whom he called a "member of the Jim Crow Pacific Coast baseball league." The thanks were for the declining performance of the team, which meant that Robinson could now park in front of his house, two blocks from the stadium. Abie Robinson also called for the Angels to consider black players who might be the Jackie Robinsons of the PCL. On February 20, 1947, he suggested in his column that the Angels sign Luther Branham, a World War II veteran and future Negro League player who had recently arrived in Los Angeles from Hawaii. Although Robinson realized that the PCL management was not likely to integrate soon, in 1947 he wrote, "We will be interested in knowing what trick the Angel ball club will use to turn him down." The *Los Angeles Sentinel* also promoted the cause to end segregation in the Pacific Coast League. On March 6, 1947, the *Sentinel* supported the conference of the Committee to End Jim Crow in Baseball.[8] The next week an editorial focused on the voice of the fans as the way to get the attention of the local ball clubs by proposing a boycott of the segregated teams: "Thousands of Negroes pay thousands of dollars every year to see the Los Angeles and Hollywood teams play and some of that money goes to every other club in the league. Perhaps a boycott is the answer." The economic power of African Americans would successfully drive many protests during the civil rights movement. In the summer of 1947 Abie Robinson suggested that the PCL could have more fans in the stands. "Our famed president [Clarence Rowland] can't see the coming of the Negro in baseball. There are 10,000 Negro baseball fans here in Los Angeles who would easily become daily patrons of Wrigley Field, within a stone's throw of the heart of the Negro community."[9]

Two other African American reporters in Los Angeles joined Abie Robinson in pressuring the PCL teams to integrate, William Claire "Halley" Harding and Herman Hill. Halley Harding played football at Washburn University, Wiley College, Fisk University, and Wilberforce University in Ohio, where he was an All-American. After playing professional basketball with the Harlem

32

Globetrotters and baseball with several Negro League teams, including the Kansas City Monarchs in the late 1920s and early 1930s, the African American athlete became a sportswriter.[10] His career as a reporter and activist included writing for the *Los Angeles Tribune* and the *Chicago New Crusader*. Harding was not just an athlete and a reporter; he was also an activist for equality. Every day he went to work prepared to challenge discrimination. He said, "I get up, shave, take a shower, dress, and then put on my boxing gloves."[11] The reporters for black presses fought every day to keep social issues in the minds of the public.

Like Halley Harding, Herman Hill was an athlete before he reported on sports. Born in Portland, Oregon, Hill broke a color barrier at the University of Southern California during the 1929–30 season by becoming the first African American to play on the varsity basketball team. Hill was also a member of the national championship track and field team in 1931 as a high jumper. After earning a bachelor's degree in business administration, Hill joined the *Pittsburgh Courier* as the West Coast editor.[12] After his journalism career Hill worked as a publicist for thirty-two years. When he died on September 1991, his obituary noted that he had also been the first African American to serve on the Los Angeles County Grand Jury.[13]

Like Harding, Herman Hill also committed himself to social justice. "You're out there and you see discrimination and injustice, and you have no choice but to use your talent and your influence to correct those wrongs. As an African American journalist, we often make news—good news—happen for our people."[14] In 1944 Hill was one of several community leaders who protested the creation of an area within the city of Los Angeles that would be black only. A City Park Commission member proposed that Watts, an area with no restrictions on black property ownership, could become a development for African Americans.[15] Hill was against this promotion of a segregated area specially designed for African Americans only. Like the editors of the black presses in the nineteenth century, Harding and Hill used their profession to agitate for change.

As the West Coast reporter for the national *Pittsburgh Courier*, Herman Hill could bring the stories of the West Coast to the nation. In 1942 he wrote about the request for a tryout for Jackie Robinson and Nate Moreland with the Chicago White Sox and the possibility of Moreland's tryout with the

Los Angeles Angels.[16] In October 1945, the month the Brooklyn Dodgers signed Jackie Robinson to a contract, a delegation that included Herman Hill and J. C. Fentress, sportswriter for the *California Eagle*, asked the Pacific Coast League Board of Directors at their regular meeting to respond to their concerns after the signing of Jackie Robinson. The delegation asked for a response to two issues: "1) Signing Negro players by Coast league clubs. 2) Allowing a new Negro league [the West Coast Baseball Association] to use Coast league facilities when teams are out of town."[17] President Clarence Rowland declined to comment and requested that the group return to the meeting on the following day. On the final day of the meeting, Rowland said that the Board of Directors would not address the two requested issues: "The subject will probably not be brought up unless some club owner so desires."[18] In November 1945 Herman Hill reported that the executives of the Pacific Coast League would "wait and see what happens" with the integration of the Dodgers.[19] By constantly bringing up the issue, Hill was reminding the PCL team owners that segregation was not acceptable. The response by Rowland also reminded the community that the owners held the decision-making power regarding integration.

Pressure on the teams in Major and Minor League Baseball by the press and the community led to several tryouts with teams at both levels during World War II. From the perspective of team management, a public tryout could appease their critics. A team could offer a tryout, which allowed the management to view the skills of the players, even when they did not intend to sign any of the players. From the perspective of the community, the players would finally get a chance to display their baseball abilities and show the team's management their skills. The community members assumed that this process would involve a fair evaluation of the players. In 1942 and 1943 tryouts with the Los Angeles Angels and the Oakland Oaks could have led to integration of the PCL before Branch Rickey signed Jackie Robinson in 1945. On December 12, 1942, the *Chicago Defender* reported that PCL president Clarence Rowland "had been observing Negro players this winter and is understood to have agreed to allow Nate Moreland, local righthand pitcher, to display his ability on the mound."[20]

Born in 1917, in Arkansas, Nathaniel Moreland played on the high school baseball team at Muir Tech High in Pasadena with Jackie Robinson. Both graduated in 1935 and continued to play baseball, now for Pasadena Junior College. In the fall of 1938 Moreland transferred to Redlands University. By the summer of 1940, Moreland played for the Baltimore Elite Giants of the Negro Leagues. In 1942 Moreland pitched for the semipro Los Angeles Colored Giants, Los Angeles Colored Athletics, and the Philadelphia Royal Colored Giants when they played in Los Angeles.[21]

Nate Moreland and Jackie Robinson petitioned the Chicago White Sox for tryouts in March 1942, while the team participated in spring training at Pasadena.[22] White Sox manager Jimmy Dykes denied the pair the opportunity for a tryout, stating, "We [managers] are powerless to act and it's strictly up to the club owners and Judge Landis [commissioner of Major League Baseball] to start the ball-a-rolling. Go after them!" Moreland's response was, "I can play in the Mexican National league, but I must fight to defend this country where I can't play!"[23] This would not be the last time Robinson or Moreland would work to overturn the color line. The exchange is also a window into who made decisions about segregation and integration. With no formal written rule about segregation in organized baseball, the commissioner and owners would be the ones to change the system. No one in Major League Baseball seemed willing to do that before Branch Rickey.

In August 1942 Hollywood Stars president Victor F. Collins said, "The hiring of Negro players would be a change in policy which would require the approval of the stockholders of the club. . . . [The hiring of black players wasn't] a matter of sufficient importance to warrant calling a meeting of the stockholders."[24] Who had the power to make the decision to integrate seemed to be in the hands of whomever the reporter was not questioning. Managers would defer to owners; owners would defer to the baseball organizational structure or to stockholders. The decision to integrate clearly resided with the owners, who decided all of the other issues related to their teams.

Moreland continued to pressure teams in Southern California, next moving to the Los Angeles Angels. In December 1942 the *Pittsburgh Courier* reported that in a meeting at Wrigley Field in Los Angeles, Clarence "Pants" Rowland, president of the Los Angeles Angels, would give Nate Moreland a tryout with the team during spring training in 1943.[25] By February 6, 1943, the tryout had not taken place, but Moreland was among the list of possible eligible African American players who lived locally. Herman Hill reported that Rowland said,

"Negro baseball players along with other nationalities whether they be Chinese, Filipino, Irish, Mexican, Jewish, or Italian, will be given full opportunity to tryout and earn berths on the Los Angeles Coast League team this spring." Rowland, a former player, manager, and scout for the Chicago White Sox, knew Philip Wrigley, the owner of the Chicago Cubs and the Los Angeles Angels, well. He was looking to Wrigley when he said, "Mr. [Philip] Wrigley is sincere and if he made such statements [about signing black players], he meant them."[26] Rowland appeared to offer spring-training tryouts in good faith, based on what he had heard from the owner of his parent organization.

Those in support of the PCL offering tryouts for blacks also worked through the Los Angeles Angels' parent organization, the Chicago Cubs. In December 1942 William L. Patterson, a lawyer, advocate for African American rights, and leader in the American Communist Party, sent a letter to Wrigley and MLB commissioner Landis to request a meeting to discuss the segregation of professional baseball. After receiving replies to both letters, Patterson scheduled a meeting with Wrigley. At the meeting in his Chicago office Wrigley listened to Patterson, who expressed his concerns that it was time "the jimcrow pattern of baseball was changed."[27] The *Chicago Defender* quoted Wrigley as saying, "I would like to see Negroes in the big leagues. I know it's got to come. But I don't think the time is now. There hasn't been enough publicity yet. What has to be done is to lay the groundwork for this by educating the public. What must be done is to get people talking. If there was sufficient demand at this time, I would put a Negro on my team now." Wrigley also expressed concern that without proper public support, fights might break out between whites and blacks during the game. Patterson responded by pointing out that football and basketball had more contact between players than baseball and fighting had not been an issue.[28]

In a second meeting with Wrigley, this time with Rowland in attendance, Patterson continued his questioning about the lack of black players in professional baseball. He recalled, "Wrigley ask[ed] Rowland if he knew of any Black baseball players who were ready for the big time. Rowland replied bluntly there were probably several, but the person he regarded as having the greatest potential was a young man who had been the most outstanding athlete at the University of California at Los Angeles. His name was Jackie Robinson."[29]

By 1943 Jackie Robinson had already captured the attention of Major League Baseball owners with his skill as an athlete. If Wrigley had signed Robinson, the history of baseball integration would have been much different. Instead, Rowland returned to California and before the 1943 season offered a tryout for the Los Angeles Angels to first baseman Lou Dials, a graduate of the University of California at Berkeley, Los Angeles resident, and then electrician at Lockheed.[30] Dials, a former Negro League player, suggested Chet Brewer, a pitcher with the Kansas City Monarchs of the Negro Leagues. Rowland extended the offer of a tryout to Brewer as well. The tryout never took place. Dials recalled Philip Wrigley as saying, "I know how good you [Dials] are, but I don't have a place for you." Dials speculated the management of the PCL was concerned that one or two black players would lead to many more and would "take over."[31]

On March 25, 1943, the *Pittsburgh Courier* reported that Clarence Rowland would not allow the tryouts to take place because so many of the farm teams for the PCL teams had folded during the war that they had an overabundance of players already under contract. The articles reported that Rowland had told black journalist Halley Harding as early as the week before that he was expecting to offer slots in spring-training camp to African Americans, but it was Angels manager Bill Sweeney who would need persuading to accept the black players.[32] While the color line was still clearly in place, no one appeared to be willing to take public responsibility for keeping it in place.

The next month another chance for integration occurred, this time with the Oakland Oaks. In April 1943 Oakland Oaks owner Vic Devincenzi offered Chet Brewer and Lou Dials a chance to tryout for his team. Herman Hill, West Coast correspondent for the *Pittsburgh Courier*; Halley Harding, *Los Angeles Tribune*; and Art Cohn, *Oakland Tribune*, had pressured Devincenzi to sign a black player. Devincenzi asked for suitable choices, and Hill and Harding offered the name of Chet Brewer.[33] Brewer and Dials joined the Oakland team during their final series against the Los Angeles Angels at Wrigley Field in Los Angeles. Oaks manager Johnny Vergez was not pleased to see the pair. When the two players arrived at the stadium, Dials recalled that the response from Vergez was "I don't know anything about it. They'll crucify me—I'll quit before I do that [allow blacks on the team]."[34] Manager Vergez phoned Oaks owner Devincenzi, they had a heated discussion, and

Vergez refused to allow the men a tryout. Devincenzi fired Vergez at the completion of the season, probably not because of this incident, and did not make any further moves to integrate.[35] In this case the person denying the black players the opportunity to play on the team was the team manager. At other times managers claimed it was not their decision, but that of the owners or commissioner. Owners and managers constantly deflected the responsibility of integration to someone else.

In April 1943, after the Los Angeles Angels denied several African American players tryouts with the team, journalists brought the issue to the Los Angeles County Board of Supervisors. Harding led the discussion during an April meeting. Supervisor Roger W. Jessup moved that the board take a firm stand in support of the athletes, which John Anson Ford seconded.[36] The *Los Angeles Times* did not report the vote.

The refusal of the Angels to offer legitimate tryouts and to sign black players led in May 1943 to action organized by Chet Brewer, Lou Dials, Halley Harding, and Herman Hill. They organized the Committee for Equal Participation in Organized Baseball.[37] With a twelve-member steering committee, the group decided to picket Wrigley Field in Los Angeles on Sunday, May 25, for the doubleheader between the Angels and the Hollywood Stars.[38] On May 15 the *Chicago Defender* reported that Los Angeles Local 887 of the United Automobile Workers and the Congress of Industrial Organizations Union of North American Aircraft Company agreed to participate in direct action against the Pacific Coast League. The union passed a resolution urging the PCL to offer tryouts "in the name of the Four Freedoms for which American boys of all races, colors and creeds are fighting and dying."[39] The white-owned *Los Angeles Times* did not note the action of fifty picketers at a game attended by nineteen thousand fans, stating only that "play was delayed half an hour because of congestion at the ticket wickets." On June 5 the black-owned *Chicago Defender* reported that fans had to walk through a picket line of people protesting the segregation of baseball. The column included a picture of the men and women on the picket line.[40] The picket did not lead to integrating the Pacific Coast League, but it did turn the feelings against segregation from talk into action.

The integration of professional baseball would formally begin in 1945. A man who had a mediocre career as a catcher, Branch Rickey changed the game of baseball as a baseball executive in two ways. First, by creating the farm system for Major League teams in the 1920s and 1930s and, then, by signing Jackie Robinson in the 1940s, Rickey helped develop the modern system of professional baseball that offered access for all players. In 1945 Rickey, the president and general manager of the Brooklyn Dodgers, devised a plan to sign an African American player. This occurred in part because of Rickey's desire to see the end of segregation in baseball, but also in response to the New York press and members of the community pressuring professional baseball. In the 1930s the communist newspaper the *Daily Worker* included a weekly sports column that became a daily sports column written by Lester Rodney. Rodney connected social criticism with his coverage of sports and published articles on the integration of baseball.[41] In the 1940s black sportswriters pressured Major League teams to hold tryouts for African American players. African American reporter Joseph Bostic, who wrote for the *New York People's Voice* as the sports editor from 1942 to 1945 as well as the *Amsterdam News*, pressured Branch Rickey by demanding tryouts for black players.[42] On Friday, April 6, 1945, Bostic approached Rickey at the Dodgers' spring-training camp at Bear Mountain, a resort south of the Catskill Mountains in upstate New York. Bostic wanted Rickey to offer tryouts to pitcher Terris McDuffie and first baseman Dave Thomas, both from the Negro Leagues. Rickey did allow the two players to try out the next day, but did not like Bostic's heavy-handedness, telling Bostic, "I am more for your cause than anybody else you know, but you are making a mistake using force."[43] Bostic applied pressure to Rickey, probably not realizing that Rickey was months away from signing a black player.

Outside of New York City *Pittsburgh Courier* reporter Wendell Smith also pressured Major League Baseball teams to sign players of color. The first African American to receive the Baseball Writers' Association of America's J. G. Taylor Spink Award for baseball writing, Wendell Smith was born June 27, 1914, in Detroit. Smith grew up playing baseball in his neighborhood and became quite a good high school player. A White Sox scout, Wish Egan, signed two local players who were white after the city high school championship game. Egan told Smith that he would have also signed him, but for his color. Wendell Smith's late wife recalled that Smith had said, "I was determined not to let that happen again."[44] The experience of exclusion from a chosen profession not because of skill but because of race would stay with Smith. In April 1945 Wendell Smith arranged a tryout for black players, this time with the Boston Red Sox. In late winter Smith contacted Isadore Muchnick, a white Boston City Council member looking for reelection in a predominately black neighborhood. Smith suggested that Muchnick should include supporting the integration of baseball in his campaign platform. If integration did not occur, Smith suggested, Muchnick would then announce that he would vote against permitting the teams to play baseball on Sunday. The reaction of the Boston Braves and Boston Red Sox was that they would have no problem signing black players and agreed to a tryout. Wendell Smith arranged for Jackie Robinson, Marvin Williams, and Sam Jethroe, all players with experience in the Negro Leagues, to participate in the tryout with the Red Sox.[45] After two days of postponements, on April 16, 1945, for about an hour starting at noon, the three men worked out for the Red Sox. Two coaches ran the tryout. *Boston Globe* sportswriter Cliff Keane remembered hearing someone shout "Get those niggers off the field" during the tryout.[46] Wendell Smith contacted Red Sox general manager Eddie Collins to follow up, but no other actions came from the Red Sox. No one would admit to shouting the epithet, although it would likely have been someone in a position to end the tryout. While the Red Sox offered a tryout, the team never intended to sign the players.[47]

After the failed Red Sox tryout, Wendell Smith went to Brooklyn to meet with Branch Rickey. Wanting to inform Rickey of the skills of Robinson, Williams, and Jethroe, Smith was surprised at Rickey's interest in Jackie Robinson. Smith left the meeting with the understanding that Rickey would evaluate the potential of Robinson to play in what Smith guessed might be an all-black league.[48] Members of the black press also pressured Major League Baseball to find a way to integrate. In the spring of 1945 the Major League owners agreed to form the Major League Committee on Baseball Integration after pressure from *Baltimore Afro-American* journalist Sam Lacy. The members included Lacy; Rickey; Larry MacPhail, the New York Yankees' general manager; and Joseph H. Rainey, a Philadelphia judge. While the committee never met and had no impact on the process of integration, it coincided with Rickey's plan to implement his "great experiment."[49]

On May 7, 1945, Rickey announced that the Brooklyn Dodgers would sponsor the Brooklyn Brown Dodgers, an all-black team that would be part of a new six-team league called the United States League. This announcement allowed Rickey to evaluate publicly African American players in the Negro Leagues. His scouts soon centered their evaluation on Jackie Robinson.[50] On October 23, 1945, Branch Rickey formally announced that the Brooklyn Dodgers would sign Jackie Robinson to a contract, not with the Brooklyn Brown Dodgers, but with the Major League team. Robinson would play the 1946 season for the Dodgers' Minor League team, the Montreal Royals. The 1946 season began with spring training in racially segregated Daytona Beach, Florida. In order to help Robinson succeed in professional baseball, Rickey also signed black pitcher John Wright, on January 29, 1946, and hired Wendell Smith to oversee the accommodations of the new black players. The rules of segregation in Florida prevented the players from staying in local hotels, so Smith turned to the black community. Wendell Smith, *Courier* photographer Billy Rowe, Jackie Robinson, and his new bride, Rachel, stayed with Viola and David Brock, while John Wright stayed across the street with A. L. Jones. Smith and Rowe became outlets for both Robinson and Wright and served as driver and secretary throughout spring training.[51]

On April 18, 1946, the first day of the regular season, Jackie Robinson played in his first game as a Montreal Royal. The Royals, a member of the International League, one of the three Triple-A leagues, provided Robinson and Rickey a chance to prove that their great experiment of integrating baseball could work. John Wright, who debuted as a Royal on April 23, 1946, and Roy Partlow, who debuted on June 5, 1946, joined Robinson on the Royals' roster.[52] The arrival of the three African Americans on the Montreal team began the process of integration of teams and other leagues. Jackie Robinson showed how African Americans could positively affect a team. In 1946 Robinson led the International League in hitting with a .349 batting average. With Robinson on the team, the Montreal Royals won not only their league championship but also the title of the Junior World Series, the World Series of the Minor Leagues.[53] In ten years with the Brooklyn Dodgers, Robinson had a Major League batting average of .311 and 197 stolen bases.[54] In his first year in Major League Baseball, Jackie Robinson was Rookie of the Year.

In 1949 he won the Most Valuable Player Award and the batting title in the National League. Robinson played in six All-Star Games between 1949 and 1954. While Jackie Robinson had a successful ten-year Major League career and was elected to the Baseball Hall of Fame in 1962, not all of the players who integrated teams would be as skilled or as lucky. John Wright and Roy Partlow would play in only thirty-seven and sixty games in Minor League Baseball, respectively. Most black players did not have careers in professional baseball; Wright and Partlow show the short time many players spent on Major or Minor League teams. The process of integration did include players who built careers in professional baseball, but there were many more who played in only a handful of games or for only a few seasons.

On May 14 the Dodgers sent John Wright to their Class C affiliate, the Trois-Rivieres (Three Rivers) Royals of the Canadian-American League. On May 23, 1946, John Wright integrated the Canadian-American League and played in his first of thirty-two games for Trois-Rivieres, finishing the season with a record of twelve wins and eight losses. After Wright spent nine seasons with Negro League teams, 1946 was his only season in the Minor Leagues.[55] Although the Dodgers also sent Partlow to Trois-Rivieres, he had more success on the diamond than Wright did. After playing in Montreal from early June to mid-July with an earned run average of 5.59, Partlow won ten of eleven games at Trois-Rivieres. Partlow attended spring training for the Royals in 1947, but did not make the team and never played in the Minors again. These two men, who were not nearly as notable as Robinson when recalling the signing of the players for the 1946 season, demonstrate the fact that integration was a process that required many people, some more successful than others, to make the whole process of social change move forward.[56]

In 1946, in addition to the Montreal Royals, the rosters of teams in three other leagues also included black players. On May 8, 1946, Roy Campanella began playing for the Class B Nashua Dodgers of the New England League. Campanella would play in Nashua for one season and then move up to Montreal in 1947. He joined the Brooklyn Dodgers in 1948 and would play in the Majors for ten years. On May 16, 1946, Don Newcombe joined Campanella in Nashua and played there for two seasons. He played for the Montreal Royals in 1948 and moved up to the Brooklyn Dodgers in 1949. Both Campanella and Newcombe had distinguished careers with the Dodgers, playing until 1957 and 1960, respectively. Roy Campanella was elected to the Baseball Hall of Fame in 1969.

An African Canadian also participated in integration in 1946. Vincent "Manny" McIntyre joined the Sherbrooke Canadians of the Class C Border League on June 3, 1946. He played thirty games in his one and only season in professional baseball. Manny McIntyre also played hockey. In the 1940s he played on semipro teams with Herbie and Ossie Carnegie. The three formed the "Black Aces," the first all-black line in professional hockey.[57] By the end of the 1946 season six black players joined four teams, integrating four different Minor Leagues. While the Brooklyn Dodgers signed Jackie Robinson first and he became the most notable player of the 1946 season, other players of color soon followed him onto team rosters. This illustrates that the process of integration is not limited to one person playing on a team, but rather many players having the opportunity and, in fact, playing. With different teams in four different leagues integrating before Jackie Robinson played one game for the Brooklyn Dodgers, the importance of the Minor Leagues in the process of integrating professional baseball should be elevated. Without the Minor Leagues to transition players from the Negro League to the Major Leagues, the integration process might not have been as successful. During the twelve-year period it took the Major Leagues to sign players of color to each of its sixteen teams, more than seventy Minor League teams integrated more than thirty-five Minor Leagues.

In 1947, the year that Jackie Robinson joined the Brooklyn Dodgers, the numbers of African Americans in the Minor Leagues increased from six players to seventeen players, integrating two additional Minor Leagues. Although this increase in numbers signaled an important change, those who played did not always stay long on the teams that signed them, sometimes playing in only one game. On May 3, 1947, Nate Moreland joined the El Centro Imperials. With the denial of tryouts with the PCL in 1942 and 1943, Moreland now crossed the color line in El Centro, California. Imperials owner George Jackson hired manager Ray Viers, a Minor League player from Ohio. Viers learned of Moreland, who was teaching at Washington Elementary School in El Centro. When Ray Viers approached George Jackson about signing Moreland, Jackson expressed concern about his color. The Viers family history recalls that Viers argued with Jackson until he was willing to accept Moreland.[58]

Nate Moreland would play ten seasons in the Minor Leagues after playing with the Baltimore Elite Giants in the Negro National League in 1940 and 1945 and the Los Angeles White Sox of the West Coast Baseball League in 1946.[59] Moreland challenged the assertion of the team owners that they could not find blacks players qualified to play for organized baseball. Denied the chance to show his abilities during World War II, Moreland would transition from the Negro Leagues to the Minors, where he would continue to build a baseball career from the age of thirty-three.

Following their success in integration in 1946, the Nashua Dodgers continued signing players of color when they added Ramon Rodriquez on May 13, 1947, to the roster the following season. Rodriquez played only one game with the Nashua Dodgers before an injury sidelined him. On July 23, 1947, the Gloversville-Johnstown Glovers became the second team of the Canadian-American League to sign an African American. Chuck Harmon, who integrated the Major League Cincinnati Reds in 1954, played in fifty-four games, with a .270 batting average. The Stamford Bombers of the Class B Colonial League signed not one or two players but six in July and August 1947. The signing of the players occurred over a two-month period when the team needed players after forfeiting a game because of a shortage. Player-manager Henry "Zeke" Bonura filled the roster with six African Americans: pitcher John Haitch (July 24, 1947), pitcher Roy Lee (July 30, 1947), pitcher Alfred Preston (August 6, 1947), infielder Carlos Santiago (August 10, 1947), pitcher Fred Shepherd (August 13, 1947), and pitcher Andreas Pulliza (August 13, 1947).[60] Although still moving in fits and starts, the process of integration continued to add new players to team rosters during the 1947 season.

In 1947 three of the sixteen Major Leagues teams integrated. The Cleveland Indians quickly followed the Brooklyn Dodgers and signed Larry Doby. Doby, the future Hall of Famer, played in his first Major League game on July 5, 1947, integrating the American League. After five years in the Negro Leagues, Doby would play another thirteen seasons in the Majors. The St. Louis Browns added to their roster Hank Thompson and Willard Brown, who both signed contracts and debuted on July 17, 1947. The Browns released Brown in August 1947 and Thompson before the 1948 season. During his career Thompson played four years in the Negro Leagues and nine in the Majors. During his first Major League season, Jackie Robinson received an extraordinary amount of attention from the press and the fans, but he was not the only player participating in a process of social change. It would take dozens of players across all levels of baseball to change the sport.

A variety of individuals and groups challenged the color line in the Pacific Coast League and in Minor League Baseball before John Ritchey joined the San Diego Padres in 1948. The managers who attempted to sign players of color before integration reminded baseball that not everyone accepted the gentlemen's agreement of segregation. Members of the press, particularly the black press, took an active role in challenging the restrictions of who could play in the PCL by pressuring teams to integrate. Even though the tryouts of the 1940s did not bring integration, the issue remained part of the public consciousness through the publication of stories about racism and segregation. Prior to the integration of the Pacific Coast League, Minor Leagues in Canada, New England, upstate New York, and Southern California signed and fielded African Americans and Latinos to play in the Minor Leagues. Four different Minor Leagues integrated before the Brooklyn Dodgers. The process of integrating baseball was varied and diverse across many teams and leagues. The Pacific Coast League was not the first league to integrate, but it would build on the successes of the teams in 1946 and 1947 and in fact would become the first league to integrate all of its teams.

CHAPTER 3

JOHN RITCHEY INTEGRATES THE
SAN DIEGO PADRES, 1948

If a Negro is good enough to stop a bullet in the Argonne Forest in
France—he is good enough to stop a line drive at Wrigley Field.
Gordon Macker, *Los Angeles Daily News*

Our interest in Ritchey is primarily that he can swing the bat. He is a
potential major league prospect and has a better than reasonable chance
of helping the Padres.
Bill Starr, San Diego Padres owner, quoted in *San Diego Union*

In 1938, with victories at the local, state, and sectional levels, the San Diego
Post 6 team traveled to Charlotte, North Carolina, to compete in the semifinals of the American Legion World Series tournament. American Legion
officials denied two black sophomores on the roster the chance to play. John
Ritchey and Nelson Manuel experienced the full force of segregation that
was common practice in the South. This was different from the racism and
discrimination in the West, which were fluid and adaptable. Ritchey experienced the flexibility of adapting racism and discrimination throughout his
life, including the integrated schools he attended and the integrated sports
team he joined. The unequal application of the rules of racism in the life of
one man is a reflection of the broader reality in the West. John Ritchey's life

included the realities of racism and discrimination in the West, which did not have stringent rules but varied, depending on the person and circumstance. By signing players of color to their rosters, Major and Minor League Baseball teams challenged the system of segregation across the country. Ritchey, a San Diego–born catcher, would begin that process in the Pacific Coast League on March 30, 1948.

John Ritchey grew up in a San Diego that exhibited its own version of the segregation and discrimination that pervaded western states. His baseball career was part of the movement for change that remade the old traditions, but his early years illustrate the challenges minorities had to negotiate in a fluid system of segregation.

John Franklin Ritchey was born January 5, 1923, in San Diego. The youngest of nine children, John was a second-generation baseball player. His father, William Herman Ritchey, moved to San Diego from Louisville, Kentucky, in 1898, and his mother, Daisy Debose, came to California from Illinois. William was catcher for the Coast Giants, a local black team for which John served as batboy.[1] "My earliest memories are of playing baseball, because there wasn't anything else to do. Most of my friends were white. . . . We played sandlot ball and the police department sponsored the league."[2] As a boy Ritchey saw the two extremes of race in baseball in that his father played on a segregated team, but young Ritchey could play with white children.

During Ritchey's childhood whites began to move out of the neighborhoods in which they had been living since the 1880s into newly built suburbs. As the whites moved out, African Americans and Mexican Americans moved in.[3] Ritchey grew up in a neighborhood in racial flux. In a 1985 interview John's older brother Bert recalled that for a time, blacks lived in neighborhoods across the city.[4] He also remembered that in the 1920s and 1930s, white home owners began to leave their old homes in urban neighborhoods for new subdivisions, and African Americans moved into those vacated areas, such as Logan Heights. Tract information from the federal census supports Bert Ritchey's recollection that African Americans resided in specific and limited areas as San Diego developed before World War II.[5] This segregated settlement pattern shows the unevenness of how San Diego practiced discrimination.

While the demographics of his neighborhood changed, young John Ritchey, a light-skinned, green-eyed African American, attended integrated schools. He played baseball and football on mixed-race teams at Memorial Junior High School and baseball at San Diego High School, graduating in 1941. "I didn't care what position I played. Just to be in the game was enough. At Memorial Junior High School I played third base, then at San Diego High I was in the outfield for two years and catcher in my last."[6] Rules dictated that African American families might not live next to white families, but their children could attend the same schools, creating practices of discrimination that blurred across aspects of society.

Despite clear lines in some areas, in some exceptional cases the fluidity of the color line in the Far West allowed some African Americans to cross the boundaries of social norms. Bert Ritchey said, "I used to go down to the downtown YMCA often. . . . I was the only black boy who was permitted in the YMCA. The YMCA's policy excluded blacks." When asked why he would receive access when other blacks did not, he said, "I was well known athletically and they just seemed to accept me. I never had anything happen while I was at the YMCA that would indicate that there was segregation, but in other words, there was a no-no for blacks."[7] Western cities, such as San Diego, practiced Jim Crow, but exceptions existed in special cases. African Americans might not know in which businesses or organizations they would perhaps face discrimination. Some places, like the YMCA, might offer exemptions to certain individuals, like successful African American athletes, but most found discrimination throughout the city. John and Bert Ritchey grew up in a city that marked them as different but created exceptions to the rules of segregation to see them play baseball. As a Southern Californian, John Ritchey had to negotiate a society that included segregation and racism. This discriminatory system, which was a product of not just the South, was also part of the heritage of the states in which Pacific Coast League teams would play: California, Oregon, and Washington.

In the nineteenth century during the period of settlement and statehood, residents in each of the three states debated the question of slavery and the role of African Americans. While the United States admitted each of the three states as free, California, Oregon, and Washington all restricted rights for minorities. California's 1849 constitution outlawed slavery, but the state laws supported the return of fugitive slaves and restricted the rights of African Americans. Several enslaved people, including Archy Lee and Bridget "Biddy" Mason, challenged their enslavement in court and won.[8] Not all Californians applied the laws of segregation in the same way; restrictions on day-to-day activities of blacks were not uniform but depended on location, regardless of the size of the minority populations. In cities such as San Francisco and larger mining towns, the population of African Americans was large enough to establish separate and restrictive lodging and restaurants. In smaller towns, however, with smaller minority populations, segregation kept African Americans confined to separate tables or sections within restaurants.[9] The southern part of the state would demonstrate strong support for the South in the Civil War.[10]

After establishing the prohibition of slavery in Oregon, an 1844 exclusion law required slave owners to free their slaves and remove them within a three-year period. Failure to remove them would mean automatic freedom for slaves.[11] White Oregonians wanted African Americans residing in the area to leave as well as to restrict the arrival of any new arrivals. Blacks who did not leave in the required time, if found guilty at trial, would receive a whipping every six months until they complied. The exclusion law reflected the sentiment of white Oregonians that there should be no blacks in the territory. In 1858, before official statehood, the people of Oregon elected a proslavery governor and proslavery congressional representatives.[12] The people of the state walked a thin line between carrying a designation of a free state while placing restrictions on minorities and not censuring proslavery leaders or sentiment. The exclusionary statutes remained part of Oregon law until the mid-1920s.[13] The effect of the discriminatory laws and racism of Oregon was a black population of only 128 in 1860.[14] African Americans did not view Oregon as a place to find financial and personal opportunities during the nineteenth century.

While California and Oregon delayed ratifying the Fifteenth Amendment, which enfranchised former slaves, Washingtonians held a different opinion. On March 26, 1870, the *Olympia Commercial Age* stated that the amendment "does not particularly affect us in this territory, as the colored folks have been voters among us for sometime already."[15] Oregon and Washington, which began as one territory, did not agree on issues of race as states. The diverging opinions are another example of how the states did not have a common practice of segregation in the nineteenth century.

During the twentieth century these beliefs would become a fluid, and frequently invisible, system of racism applied through legal and social means throughout the Pacific Coast states.[16] The 1910s and early 1920s included race riots and protests. During this period restrictive racial codes became law, supported by real estate organizations such as the National Association of Real Estate Boards.[17] In addition to restriction of home ownership, blacks faced racism in the day-to-day practices of business in California; segregation of public spaces demonstrated the racial biases of the state. In the summer of 1912 a black Los Angelina wrote a letter to the *Crisis*, the newsletter of the National Association for the Advancement of Colored People, in which she illustrated the segregation she faced regularly: "We suffer almost anything (except lynching) right here in the beautiful land of sunshine. Civil privileges are unknown. You can't bathe at the beaches, eat in any first-class place, nor will the street car and sight-seeing companies sell us tickets if they can possibly help it. I am speaking from experience."[18]

African Americans in the West had to negotiate a path between what the law stated and social reality. The town in which John Ritchey grew up was no exception. In 1934 in San Diego blacks began moving into previously all-white residential areas in the southeastern part of the city.[19] The geographical location did not overturn other discriminatory practices. Blacks could enter and sit in a local restaurant, but once inside employees either did not serve them or harassed them. A San Diegan said of the time, "California had a civil rights law, but nobody observed it. . . . I found out many people had filed suits against restaurants here, but nobody had ever won one."[20] The practices of the local business and the reality of people's lives differed. Regardless of laws on the books, California could be as restrictive as other regions of the country that had a longer and more entrenched formal system of segregation.

Even though the rules of segregation in San Diego bent to allow him to play on integrated baseball teams in junior high and high school, John Ritchey faced rigid lines of segregation when he played outside of the region. He and fellow African American teammate Nelson Manuel experienced discrimination as part of the American Legion National Junior Baseball Tournament, a prestigious sporting event for high school athletes.[21] Founded in 1925, the American Legion Baseball Program worked to instill American values in young boys. Ironically, it did just that. While they faced no discrimination while playing in California, Ritchey and Manuel would experience a strict and rigid system of segregation in the South.

In August 1938 the two men traveled with their teammates to Charlotte to play in the semifinal series of the national tournament. The team from San Diego had already played across Southern California, in Northern California, and in Grand Forks, North Dakota. The team traveled by train, and they faced rigid travel problems, hotel restrictions, and teams that did not want to play against them because of their mixed-race roster.[22] As the teams prepared for the series in Charlotte, the organizers denied the two black players the right to play in the semifinals or finals.[23] The two sophomores must have been confused and angry when Coach Dewey "Mike" Morrow informed them of the league's decision. Morrow decided to play without Ritchey and Manuel. The Post 6 team beat Detroit in the semifinals, but lost to Spartanburg, South Carolina, in the finals. How must the two excluded players have felt when they returned to San Diego as part of a team that had played the final series without them? Ritchey and Manuel had learned to negotiate the lines of discrimination in San Diego, because for well-liked, quality athletes, those lines frequently bent and blurred. In the South of the 1930s, however, the rules could not be broken.

Two years later, in August 1940, the San Diego Post 6 team returned to the national tournament. From a initial field of twenty-three thousand teams, the competition came down to four teams.[24] John Ritchey and Nelson Manuel, now seniors, again played with their teammates on the San Diego Post 6 team as it won each level of the tournament, from local games in San Diego to a regional championship in Arizona to the western title in St. Louis. They again reached the semifinals, which in 1940 were in Shelby, North Carolina. San Diego faced a team from the St. Louis Aubuchon-Dension Post. Expecting segregation to exclude Ritchey and Manuel, Coach Morrow expressed surprise when the tournament allowed him to play his entire team in the semifinals. Ritchey and Manuel played in the semifinal round, becoming the first African Americans ever to play whites in this southern tournament.[25] Playing before three thousand fans in the first game of the series, San Diego beat St. Louis 5–4. In his column "Talking It Over," *San Diego Evening Tribune* sports editor Tom Akers offered this view of that landmark game for fans back home: "No hint of objection was heard from any quarter. In fact, the spectators showed a generous, sportsmanlike spirit that was both gratifying and surprising. . . . It is related that each time the boys came to bat, the assembled thousands cheered lustily."[26]

Ritchey and Manuel offered a much different version of the game, however. They stated that St. Louis players played fair, but the crowd shouted epithets such as "nigger, snowball, sunshine, and coon."[27] The reality on the field was much different from the reality constructed by the white sports editor. In the same column Akers wrote of the history-making game:

> Win, lose, or draw, the American Legion's Junior baseball team representing Post Six of San Diego has accomplished what might be called a miracle. It has, for the first time that these competitions began in the "deep South," sent a team upon the field in which there were Negro players. In so doing, the California team upset all precedent and surmounted prejudice deep-rooted in the traditions of a section of the country long steeped in those sentiments. So the action of those in charge of the play in Shelby, N.C., must be accepted as progressive, broad-minded and liberal to an astonishing extent. We must not forget that we of the far west look on matters of this nature in a different light from the residents of the southern states. California parents have not the slightest objection to their son taking part in athletic competitions against Negroes.[28]

Akers's comments claimed the West had more enlightened attitudes that those who upheld the formal segregation of the South. His vision extended only so far: while black children in San Diego could play on integrated teams, as Ritchey had, the parents of their white teammates chose not to live next door to his family. While the racial realities practiced in the West may not have been the same as in the South, nonwhites still faced racism and discrimination in their daily lives. Akers's enthusiasm for this moment of social change was short-lived, however, because the rules of segregation reappeared in the final series of the tournament.

The night before San Diego was to play the first of a best-of-five series against the Albemarle Legionnaires in Albemarle, North Carolina, A. K.

Wingate, president of the Efird Mills, a local textile manufacturing company, told Coach Mike Morrow that the organization would not allow him to play Ritchey and Manuel. When Morrow asked why, Wingate responded that a riot would ensue. The next morning the sheriff, who said he had consulted with the district attorney, also tried to influence Morrow. Morrow argued, "They are two of my best players. They played in Shelby, N.C. last week. I didn't see any riots."[29] Morrow pressed for the use of the two black seniors. "Either my two colored boys will play in the junior World Series or we go back to San Diego."[30] According to the rules of the tournament, since the team from San Diego was ready, willing, and able to play and since the team from Albemarle was not, Albemarle should have forfeited the game. However, officials tried to construct a deal. At first Morrow compromised by agreeing not to start the two black players, but wanted to retain the option to play them if needed during the game.

When Morrow did not agree to remove Ritchey and Manuel from his roster, the American Legion leadership became involved. Homer Chaillaux, the legion's National Junior Baseball chairman and Americanism chairman, sent a telegram to Dr. Roy French Kidd, the Post 6 commander, stating that the national office forbade the two black players from playing in the finals. The telegram simply stated, "Negroes Nelson Manuel and John Ritchey will not play in the opener today of the championship series with Albemarle at Albemarle, N.C., very much south of the Mason-Dixon Line." Chaillaux did not make a public statement about the decision to exclude the players, but his telegram shows his support for segregation.[31] The San Diego post commander agreed to the withdrawal of the two players, and eventually Morrow acquiesced. "It happened to us in 1938 and we won anyway. I had hoped it wouldn't come up again, but this time it did."[32]

While Ritchey and Manuel had played in the semifinals in Shelby, the tournament would not allow them in the finals the following week in Albemarle. In response to Morrow's challenge against restricting Ritchey and Manuel in the finals, arguing that they had already played in the semifinals, tournament officials responded by saying that in the semifinals San Diego played against a team from the North and the fans had little interest in the game.[33] That attempt by tournament officials to give a reason the black players were allowed to play in the semifinals but not the finals fell short for the San Diego team. The decision against Ritchey and Manuel appeared to be a tournament-level decision, supported by the American Legion, at both the local and the national levels. White journalist Art Cohn published his opinion about the matter: "Albemarle protested and the boys were declared ineligible because they had committed the crime of being born black. Without these two key players, San Diego lost the title. This happened in the championship series of a tournament sponsored by the *American* Legion."[34] While the players had supporters who championed their cause, it would not change the outcome.

In the end the games went on without Ritchey or Nelson. Dressed in their uniforms, they watched the opening ceremonies and the game from the dugout. In the *Charlotte Observer*, sportswriter Jake Wade described boos from people in the stands as Ritchey and Manual completed their warm-ups. "I was taking batting practice in Albemarle before the game when we learned we couldn't play. In those days, you just did as the adults told you to do."[35] The San Diego team lost Game Five 9–8 in front of fourteen thousand fans. As a teenager in a junior tournament, Ritchey broke ground when he and Manuel integrated the American Legion semifinals in 1940.

John Ritchey had faced discrimination growing up in San Diego, but until he traveled to North and South Carolinas, he had not experienced the full force of Jim Crow. The rules in the West were not as rigid as the South, as no one had ever denied Ritchey the right to play in a baseball game with his team in San Diego. Ritchey did not yet know that he would integrate the PCL, but he got a taste of what was to come. He had faced discrimination and segregation in San Diego, but the experience of the American Legion banning him from the semifinals and finals in South Carolina in 1938 and the finals in North Carolina in 1940 must have brought the reality of racism to a new level for Ritchey, one that highlights the varied ways that different regions of the country applied segregation. The young man who had access to unsegregated classrooms and baseball diamonds in his hometown of San Diego must have felt the full force of segregation when denied access to all levels of the tournament in the South.

In 2007 a photograph of the San Diego American Legion Post 6 team emerged. The team photo, taken before the 1940 American Legion World Series games, included both John Ritchey and Nelson Manuel. In the photo

John Ritchey is looking at the ground, his chin on his hand, which rests on his knee, and his cap covers his face. While the photographer may just have caught Ritchey at an inopportune moment, it may also be visual evidence of how the seventeen-year-old must have felt being excluded from the tournament for a second time.

Baseball continued to be part of John Ritchey's life as he looked for work after graduating from San Diego High School. In the summer of 1941 Ritchey worked in the same National Youth Administration program as Jackie Robinson. At a camp in Atascadero, about two hundred miles north of Los Angeles, they played baseball against other semipro teams to entertain campers and work with disadvantaged children. Due to financial problems the program did not last long. In August 1947 Ritchey remembered their time together in 1941 and said of his teammate, "Robinson was a swell ballplayer then and I wasn't surprised he was signed by the Dodgers. He is without a doubt the greatest player I ever saw."[36] This statement came, of course, in the middle of Robinson's experimental 1947 season.

In 1942 Ritchey began his studies at San Diego State College. The school paper, the *Aztec*, reported that Ritchey turned down several offers to play with teams in the Negro Leagues, choosing instead to attend college.[37] As a freshman Ritchey played again on an integrated team, beginning the season playing both left field and catcher, one of only two freshmen to start for the Aztecs.[38] Successful and popular, Ritchey hit .444 in fifty-four at bats during the 1942 season. Coach Charlie Smith's undefeated San Diego State team defeated the Fresno State team for the California Collegiate Athletic Association Championship.[39] San Diego fans appeared willing to evaluate Ritchey on his baseball skills rather than his skin color. As a local San Diegan who could bring the local college team victories, Ritchey found acceptance on the team. Again, this acceptance demonstrated the varied degrees of acceptance of African Americans by the larger white community. Ritchey, a successful and popular baseball player, was seen as a role model, as indicated by his "Pops" nickname.

Like many others, John Ritchey was drafted by the U.S. Army in 1943. As one of the more than 1.2 million African Americans who served in World War II, Ritchey served in a segregated noncombat unit. Ritchey traveled overseas with the 1323rd Engineer General Service Regiment in Europe and the Philippines. Ritchey was part of the Normandy campaign, arriving in France on July 7, 1944. Five members of his regiment rest in the American Cemetery and Memorial in Normandy. Members of the 1323rd entered Germany on April 1, 1945. In July the regiment traveled from Marseilles to Manila, Philippines, through the Strait of Gibraltar and the Panama Canal on the ss *Brazil*. Of his service Ritchey said, "Our outfit? Combat and construction. Mostly building bridges. . . . [W]e went through the Normandy campaign. And the Battle of the Bulge. By v-e day we were in the suburbs of Berlin."[40] The army discharged Ritchey as a staff sergeant with five battle stars. Like so many other veterans, John Ritchey returned home after serving his country looking ahead to the future.

The country was changing as so many service members like Ritchey returned home. Civil rights and equality were becoming part of the national discussion. On March 2, 1945, the case that would become *Mendez v. Westminster* was filed in federal court. The Mendez family joined others in protesting the segregation of their children in several school districts in Orange County, California. The appeal was argued in 1946. The Ninth Circuit Court of Appeals issued a decision in favor of the families on April 14, 1947.[41] Also in California, the November 1946 ballot included Proposition 11, a measure that would create the Fair Employment Practices Commission and make it illegal for employers to discriminate because of race, religion, color, national origin, or ancestry, and Proposition 15, an amendment that would validate changes made by the state legislature to the 1920 Alien Land Law. Both propositions were defeated.[42] On December 5, 1946, President Harry Truman signed Executive Order 9808, establishing the President's Committee on Civil Rights, which had the task of investigating the conditions of civil rights and making recommendations to improve them. Issues of civil rights were also appearing in sports.

When Ritchey returned to California in 1946, he resumed his studies at San Diego State College. He also continued to play baseball under Coach Charlie Smith. Jim Gleason, a white college teammate who would play in the PCL in 1947, remembered Ritchey:

As a youth in San Diego, I had two idols: Ted Williams and John Ritchey. Teammates respected him, because he brought so much experience to

San Diego State. Watching Ritchey when he was a teenager was an inspiration, Johnny had a great talent for the game, which he enhanced by his enthusiastic attitude. He loved the game and played with a big, happy smile on his face. He was Johnny Baseball. I learned more from him than anybody in baseball. He'd concentrate and make you concentrate. He was the first guy who taught me intensity. He'd say "we can work together." He gave you confidence.[43]

This memory of Ritchey as always smiling and upbeat is important, because Gleason would watch Ritchey's career develop and later note how being the player who integrated a professional league affected the player he called Johnny Baseball. Playing on integrated teams for San Diego State did not seem to weigh down Ritchey. He met his future wife, Lydia, the year he reenrolled in San Diego State. At age twenty-three, with a family now in his future, he needed to make a steady income to support a family. Ritchey turned to playing professional baseball. In 1946 the only option in professional baseball available to Ritchey was the Negro Leagues. In March 1947 Ritchey boarded a train with fellow San Diegans Jessie "Sailor" Williams and Walter McCoy and headed east to play for the Negro League team the Chicago American Giants. Lydia did not go with him because, as she explained in an interview, her father was a minister, and he would not allow it before their marriage. John and Lydia did speak on the phone regularly, and he mailed her newspaper clippings that would become the scrapbook of his career.[44]

The Negro Leagues offered Ritchey the opportunity to earn a living playing professional baseball. In 1947, Ritchey's rookie year, the Chicago American Giants had a win-loss record of 31-50. Ritchey had a much better year. He won the batting title with a .381 average. His debut in Comiskey Park in Chicago came on April 27, 1947, in a doubleheader Sunday exhibition game against the Cleveland Buckeyes. He had beaten out veteran catcher Jake Tolbert for the position of starting catcher with his "powerful hitting and errorless play behind the plate."[45] The five-foot-ten, 172-pound twenty-four-year-old had hit above .300 on every team on which he had ever played. Chicago in 1947 was to be no exception. Yet while he was on familiar ground on the baseball diamond, the young man from San Diego had entered a new world of race relations. Many of the players on Negro League teams came from the South and had experience with Jim Crow. The cities of the Midwest and the East to which the Giants traveled also had larger African American communities than Ritchey played for in San Diego.

The season for the Chicago American Giants began in Kansas City on May 4, 1947. The press had predicted the pitching of Al Gipson would rejuvenate the Giants that season, but it was the rookie Ritchey who would play a central role in the successes of the year. Five weeks into the season, Ritchey had 46 at bats, 12 runs, 17 hits, 6 runs batted in, and a .370 average. Articles in the *Chicago Defender* praised Ritchey's skill and future in baseball. By July 15, 1947, Ritchey had played in fifty-eight games with 176 at bats, 42 runs, and 67 hits, batting .381. Though his statistics harked back to his days in San Diego, Ritchey was a long way from his western home. His wife recalled that his African American teammates did not fully accept him, both because of his light skin and because of his not having grown up under the same racial restrictions as they had. "Players called him, 'That green-eyed ballplayer from California.'"[46] Coming from the West, rather than the South or the East, set Ritchey apart from the other players of the Negro Leagues.

As John Ritchey proved himself as a professional baseball player, others already saw the potential for him to play in the Major Leagues. In August 1947 Ritchey's batting average was .367. Wendell Smith wrote a *Pittsburgh Courier* column highlighting Ritchey as a good Major League prospect. As a promoter of integration, Wendell had his eye on Ritchey as the player who might break the barrier in Chicago, on either the Cubs or the White Sox. To Smith's question, Ritchey said he would welcome a chance for a tryout by either the Sox or the Cubs: "After all, every ball player would like to play in the majors. I don't know if I could make the grade, but I would sure like the chance."[47] Ritchey was a member of the first generation of African American baseball players who saw the real possibility of making it to the Majors. After years of segregation, once Jackie Robinson opened the door, there was a chance to play at the Major League level, and Ritchey wanted to take it.

Team owners outside of Negro League baseball noted John Ritchey's skills on the diamond. On September 19, 1947, Ritchey participated in a tryout for the Chicago Cubs. He worked out with fifty other hopefuls for three Chicago Cubs scouts.[48] In attendance were Chicago American Giants owner and Negro American League president J. B. Martin and *Chicago Defender* sports editor Fay Young. Those who saw him viewed Ritchey as a candidate for Class A or B if signed. One article stated he was certainly going to report to the Cubs' spring training in 1948. When asked if he would be willing to sell Ritchey's contract to the Major League Chicago Cubs, Martin said, "I think we will be able to work out something, if the Cubs are interested. When they asked him to report today, however, they did not say anything about buying his contract. We'll have to wait and see what develops."[49] Harold George of the Cubs said, "Ritchey did 'all right' and might be a good prospect. He can move fast for a catcher and has a good arm."[50] In an interview with Wendell Smith, George was not sure what the Cubs intended to do with Ritchey but said, "All I can say now is that we have an interest in him and that is why we had him work out." In a *Chicago Defender* article in April 1948, columnist Fay Young said Ritchey did not want to go to a Minor League team, "failed to follow instructions from the Cubs' office and this winter signed with the San Diego Padres."[51] Maybe it was the lure of returning home to San Diego, the insistence of his future bride, or the assurance of a professional baseball contract, but Ritchey's next move was to the PCL.

During the fall of 1947 J. B. Martin was talking with San Diego Padres owner Bill Starr. At issue was Ritchey's contract with Martin's team. Like other Negro League players, his Negro Leagues contract, or lack of contract, became an issue for Ritchey. In his column Wendell Smith said the contract issue was the proof that "most Negro League clubs are operated on a slip-shod basis." Smith went on to describe the controversy surrounding Ritchey's attempt to join the Padres: "The signing set off a growl and a roar in the vicinity of Chicago. J. B. Martin . . . charged that the San Diego club had stolen Ritchey from him. He immediately dispatched a letter of protest to Major League Baseball Commissioner Happy Chandler. He demanded an investigation."[52] However, the investigation centered on an examination of Ritchey's supposed contract with the Giants, which neither Martin nor manager "Candy Jim" Taylor could produce. Martin pleaded that Ritchey had played for him all year, albeit without a contract, but the commissioner would not support his cause.

On November 22, 1947, John Franklin Ritchey signed with his hometown team, the San Diego Padres. At a ceremony similar to the October 23, 1945, signing of Jackie Robinson, a photo of the event shows Ritchey signing his contract with owner Bill Starr smiling behind him. The focus for San Diegans was not his success as a Negro League ballplayer, but the return of a hometown player well known from his San Diego High School and San Diego State days. However, in many ways John Ritchey's year in Chicago helped legitimize him as the player to integrate the PCL because it gave him experience as a professional baseball player. Ritchey's time in Chicago also provided others, such as Starr, the opportunity to evaluate Ritchey's ability to play baseball.

Bill Starr, a former catcher, was born in Brooklyn in 1911 and raised in Chicago. He played professional baseball in 1931 and in the Nebraska State League, the Minor Leagues, and with the Major Leagues' Washington Senators in 1935.[53] He ended his career as a San Diego Padre in 1939. Starr became principal owner of the Padres in 1944 and was a baseball innovator until 1955. In his book *Clearing the Bases: Baseball Then and Now*, Starr does not mention John Ritchey or anything about integration. He does recall acquiring Tom Alston, the African American first baseman, and selling Alston's contract to the St. Louis Cardinals for the largest price ever paid for a Minor League player. Alston integrated the St. Louis Cardinals in April 1954, but Starr makes no mention of Alston's part in baseball history.

When Bill Starr signed John Ritchey to his Pacific Coast League contract, he declared to a group of sportswriters, photographers, and club officials that he was not supporting any cause. "Our interest in Ritchey is primarily that he can swing the bat. He is a potential major league prospect and has a better than reasonable chance of helping the Padres."[54] In an interview with the *Chicago Defender* in 1950, Starr did state, "Of course, we were aware of the implications. But the main thing is: we were looking for good players. We knew of Ritchey . . . because he lives here. To sign him was the obvious thing to do." In the West Starr was able to see past a player's skin color to his skills on the diamond, something most baseball managers and owners could not or were not willing to do during the previous sixty years. While Starr may have appeared to be on the forefront of social change, signing a successful black player could also mean financial gains. Of the fans in San Diego, Starr said, "Fans go to games as a form of escape and to be entertained. They are not too much interested in sociological problems. It's been proven that baseball prejudice is a surface thing. All the fans want is a good ball game. They want to see good players, regardless of race."[55] While Starr's opinion may be either naive or Pollyannaish, he would not have made those statements if he did not feel the fans would support the black players.

When asked about Ritchey's arrival, manager Jimmy "Rip" Collins felt there would be no problems. "Of course not. And there won't be any, either. Those days are gone. John is a member of the team and will remain a member unless we decide he needs a season or so of farming." Ritchey also described a welcoming reception: "I couldn't ask for a better setup. When I came to town Collins greeted me warmly, introduced me to the other fellows and then told me to go out and do a good job. There hasn't been an incident of any kind and I'm getting the exact amount of attention all the other players are getting. I played Legion ball with a number of fellows on the club and we've been friends for years. It's all been so good I can hardly believe it."[56] Of course, all parties were portraying the situation in the best possible way to help the experiment succeed.

The San Diego Padres were one of a number of teams experimenting with integration. In 1948 there were forty-eight different Minor Leagues across six levels of skill. During that season, more than fifteen other players of color had joined teams in six different Minor Leagues. The PCL would be the second Triple-A Minor League to begin integrating, followed by the third, the American Association, less than two months later. In addition to the PCL and the American Association, four other Minor Leagues integrated in 1948. The Pennsylvania-Ontario–New York (Pony) League, the Middle Atlantic League, the Eastern League, and the Central League each had a team that signed a player of color for the first time. Four leagues, the New England League, the International League, the Central League, and the Provincial League, signed players of color to new teams, adding new teams to those already integrated. Six of the ten teams that integrated in that year had an affiliation with either the Brooklyn Dodgers or the Cleveland Indians, both Major League teams that integrated in 1947. Even though the PCL was not the first league to integrate one of its teams, they would become the first to integrate all of their eight teams.

To succeed in integration John Ritchey needed a structure of support. On February 1, 1948, before the start of spring training for the 1948 baseball season, he married Lydia Quinn. They lived in an apartment in Ontario,

California, during spring training. He said, "Everyone's been swell to me, I couldn't ask for better treatment. In exhibition games, most of the customers were on my side, and the umpires offered me all kinds of encouragement. All the players have cooperated with me. . . . To be perfectly frank, I did expect a little friction, but I haven't encountered any." A newspaper article noted the sign of Ritchey's full acceptance was when Jake Wade, the pitcher from North Carolina, chose Ritchey to warm him up to pitch. When Bill Starr signed the catcher, he contacted each of the team's road hotels. All six said that Ritchey would be able to stay without any problem. The manager of San Francisco's Alexander Hamilton Hotel said, "If he is good enough to play on your team, he is more than welcome at our hotel."[57]

John Ritchey began his Padre career with a pinch hit in a game against Los Angeles at Wrigley Field. When the team returned to San Diego, Ritchey hit safely seven times in his first eleven at bats at Lane Field. "It was a thrill to play for the Padres. The fans cheered and my feeling was it was because I was a San Diego boy making good. It had nothing to do with race. A lot of friends and family members were in the stands at Lane Field. It felt good just to get a turn at bat, but I grounded out to the first basemen."[58] Third baseman Lou Estes said, "Something that really impressed me about John was that it didn't make any difference what bat he used. It could be a thirty-three or a thirty-six. You know how choosey hitters are about what bat they use. I said, 'John, why don't you use the same bat?' He said, 'It doesn't matter. You can hit with all of them.' He'd just walk up to the plate and get his hits."[59] John Ritchey had the skills needed to succeed in the Minor Leagues.

Much as Ritchey had not found complete acceptance from his Negro League teammates, life as a Padre brought Ritchey some of the same treatment that black players endured in integrating the Major League teams: taunts from rival teams, rooming alone on road trips, eating without the company of a teammate.[60] Ritchey never complained about the slights, but it did bother him that his teammates would not retaliate for him on the baseball field. He recalled:

One time I was coming home and the catcher tried to spike me in the leg as I came sliding under him. . . . They didn't throw at me more than they did at white players, but some pitchers did. There was an Angel who threw four balls at my head. I took first. My teammates said nothing and there was no retaliation. Another time against the Angels, I got a double. The pitcher came to second base. He was spitting and yelling all kinds of bad language in my face. Then he left the game. Nobody said or did anything and I was lonely. I had to room alone, but I was never refused accommodations in the PCL.[61]

Jimmie Reese, a Major League second baseman, coached and for a short period managed for the Padres in 1948. He said, "Bill Starr brought in John Ritchey and some of the early black players. It was hard to adjust right away. The same situation occurred when Rickey brought Robinson in. People like [Minnie] Minoso [*sic*], [Harry "Suitcase"] Simpson, and [Luke] Easter helped speed the acceptance of black players—no doubt about it. They were handicapped to start with and now it's accepted without any problem. They're a part of baseball and have played a big part, I'll tell you that."[62]

While the public face of the San Diego Padres welcomed players of color, the day-to-day realities did not always live up to the sentiments of the press conferences. The players were willing to accept the costs to their part in the integration of baseball, but it would cost them individually.

John Ritchey may not have expressed the pressures he felt as the league's first black player, but his former San Diego State teammate Jim Gleason said that the pressure seemed to take a toll on Ritchey's trademark smile and joy of the game:

> The pressure on Johnny was intense. Playing with him for a short while on the Padres and later against him in the Texas League, I saw a transition. He brought that same enthusiasm, sparkle, and talent to the Padres. He also carried a tremendous burden being the first black player in the PCL, and, later, in the Texas League. I'm taking nothing away from Jackie Robinson who was tougher, less sensitive, and more of a fighter. Johnny was a very sensitive guy, a real team player and when some of his teammates treated him differently, Johnny felt this intensely. I never observed hostility, but I did observe a coolness, a distancing that was very apparent to Johnny. The smile on his face disappeared. Playing was not what it used to be for "Johnny Baseball." Now he was only contributing to the team and the game what you read in the box scores. Those statistics fell

because the game he loved and the team spirit that buoyed him to better performance had now become burdensome and diluted his exceptional talent. At another time, Johnny would have been a major leaguer. He was tremendous. A few years later, it would have been easier for him, but Johnny made it easier for others.[63]

This change, seen by a teammate who watched him play over several years, showed the effects of racism on an individual. In the day-to-day struggle of facing discrimination, trying to earn a living, and being a model for his race, John Ritchey felt the toll over time, and it changed him. Jim Gleason had a seven-year career in Minor League Baseball. He understood the pressures of the game. In Ritchey Gleason saw the man change as he carried the weight of being a racial pioneer onto the baseball diamond each day. Professional baseball, a difficult game to play in the best of circumstances, was a challenging career, but even more so for those who also represented their race and played a role in changing society.

John Ritchey played 103 games as a San Diego Padre in 1948. He hit .323 with an on-base percentage of .405. In 217 at bats, Ritchey had 70 hits and 4 home runs. Ritchey avoided going to the Western International League and by the end of the season secured a starting position for the 1949 season.

As John Ritchey helped change baseball as one of the players on an integrated team, American society continued to change as well. In January the Supreme Court issued two decisions related to race. First, in *Sipuel v. Board of Regents of University of Oklahoma*, in a unanimous decision the court stated that Oklahoma could not deny Lois Ada Sipuel, an African American, entrance to law school solely because of her race. In *Oyama v. California* the Supreme Court decided that certain provisions of the 1913 and 1920 California Alien Land Laws abridged rights guaranteed in the Fourteenth Amendment. In May in *Shelley v. Kramer* the Supreme Court issued a ruling that said that courts could not enforce racial covenants. Just a month later, in *Takahashi v. Fish and Game Commission*, the court said that the requirement of American citizenship for a fishing license was unreasonable and discriminatory to Japanese Americans, who would not be able to become naturalized American citizens until 1952. On July 26 President Harry Truman issued Executive Orders 9980 and 9981, which desegregated the federal workforce and desegregated the military, respectively. On October 1 the California Supreme Court overturned the state's ban on interracial marriage when it decided in favor of Andrea Perez, a Mexican American woman, and Sylvester Davis, an African American man, who had applied for a marriage license in Los Angeles.[64] In December 1948 the administrator of the Civil Aeronautics Administration desegregated the nation's only federally owned airport, National Airport, in Washington DC. These Supreme Court decisions, presidential actions, and federal pronouncements joined with the integration of sport in changing American society.

John Ritchey made PCL history when he played in his first game as a San Diego Padre on March 30, 1948. The catcher who had grown up in San Diego had experienced twenty-five years of a system of racial segregation that was fluid and varied, but one that had developed from the earliest years of each of the states along the Pacific Coast. As integration in Minor League Baseball began to take hold, it offered new opportunities for players of color in professional baseball. John Ritchey would be the first of many players who would play baseball and be part of a movement for changing American society.

CHAPTER 4

MOMENTUM AND CHALLENGES, 1949

Everybody likes me when I hit that ball.

Luke Easter to Bill Starr, quoted in *Chicago Defender*

When the San Diego Padres opened their season against the Hollywood Stars on March 31, 1949, the team roster included a new player. The six-foot-four, 240-pound first baseman arrived in San Diego under contract from the Padres' Major League affiliate, the Cleveland Indians. While he claimed to be twenty-seven, the thirty-four-year-old already had two years of professional experience with the Homestead Grays. San Diego Padres owner Bill Starr remembered, "He was the most phenomenal gate attraction ever to hit the Pacific Coast League, and I am not excluding Joe DiMaggio."[1] In just eighty games with the Padres, Luke Easter would hit twenty-five home runs and break attendance records across the league. When Bill Starr first met with Luke Easter to talk with him about the prejudice he might face, Easter replied, "Mr. Starr, when I hit a baseball, everybody likes me. It's what happens on the field that counts."[2] Easter showed the PCL owners that many fans were more interested in the quality of players than their skin color. Fans might put aside their prejudices to see a player hit home runs. During the 1949 season three additional PCL teams added players of color to their rosters, and the momentum of integration became more than just one player.

By the 1949 season integration in baseball had moved beyond signing a single player to a team to adding multiple players. In the Major Leagues, the Brooklyn Dodgers' roster now included Jackie Robinson, Roy Campanella, and Don Newcombe. The rosters of three other Major League teams, the Cleveland Indians, the St. Louis Browns, and the New York Giants, each included more than one player of color. Minor League teams also continued to add black and Latino players to their rosters. Integration had now gained enough forward momentum that opponents would have a difficult time stopping the process. As team owners began to reap financial gains from the success and popularity of the new additions to their teams, they signed more players of color. Integration was not without problems, though, as individual owners or managers could still choose not to sign players or treat the players differently because of their race rather than their baseball skills or abilities. Teams set quotas of the number of players of color they would allow on their rosters.

In 1949, just the second year of integrated play for the PCL, half of the league—the San Diego Padres, Oakland Oaks, Portland Beavers, and Los Angeles Angels—all included players of color on their rosters. In 1949 the San Diego Padres signed Afro-Cuban Minnie Miñoso, and the Portland Beavers signed Panamanian Frank Austin and Puerto Rican–born Luis Márquez. The signing of these three players included dark-skinned Latinos as well as African Americans in the integration process. Each of these three players came to the PCL from the Negro Leagues. The transition from the Negro Leagues to organized baseball brought contractual issues that required new agreements between the two groups. During the 1949 season more teams in the Minor Leagues integrated than in the Major Leagues.

While Branch Rickey led the initial foray into integration, the Major Leagues did not remain on the forefront. In 1949 only one new Major League team integrated, and it signed two players. The New York Giants added Monte Irvin and Hank Thompson to their roster on July 8, 1949. Future Hall of Famer Irvin played nine seasons in the Negro Leagues before going between the Majors and Minors for two seasons. He played in professional baseball for another seven seasons, ending his career in the Pacific Coast League in 1957. After playing four seasons in the Negro Leagues, Thompson played in the Minor Leagues for parts of three seasons and nine seasons in the Majors. Thompson's professional baseball career ended with the Triple-A Minneapolis Millers in 1957. The Minor Leagues continued to play an important role in the integration of the Major Leagues. Many players of color began or ended their careers with a Minor League team, and Major League teams could send players to the Minors for more experience.

As the Major Leagues integrated at a measured pace, the Minors did so more quickly. In 1948 in addition to the PCL, at least five other Minor Leagues integrated. In 1949 four new Minor Leagues added players of color to their rosters. The ability of a Minor League team to integrate was sometimes tied to the integration status of its Major League affiliate. Since the Minor League team would look to the Major League team for players to add to its roster, if the parent team had not integrated, it would not have any players of color to send to play on the farm team.

In the Pacific Coast League teams integrated with three kinds of affiliation with Major League teams: no affiliation, affiliation with a Major League team that had not yet integrated, and affiliation with a Major League team that had integrated. None of the first three PCL teams to integrate, the San Diego Padres, the Oakland Oaks, and the Portland Beavers, had a formal affiliation with a Major League team when they integrated. The late 1940s and early 1950s were a time of establishing the relationship between Major League teams and Minor League affiliates. Many of the black players who played in the Pacific Coast League would move up to the affiliated Major League team. By the start of the 1949 season Bill Starr had affiliated the Minor League San Diego Padres with the Major League Cleveland Indians. Both Luke Easter and Minnie Miñoso would play for Cleveland in 1949. In 1951 Sam Hairston moved from the Sacramento Solons to its Major League team, the Chicago White Sox. The Los Angeles Angels and the Major League Chicago Cubs, both owned by Philip K. Wrigley, had formalized an affiliate relationship, and Gene Baker moved from the Los Angeles Angels to integrating the Chicago Cubs along with Ernie Banks on September 14, 1953. For some Minor League teams, the relationship with an affiliate team influenced the process of integration.

After the first three PCL teams integrated, the next five teams, the Los Angeles Angels, the Sacramento Solons, the San Francisco Seals, the Hollywood Stars, and the Seattle Rainiers, all had a Major League affiliate when they integrated. Three of the four PCL teams integrated before their Major League affiliates—the Los Angeles Angels (1949) and Chicago Cubs (1953), Sacramento Solons (1949) and Chicago White Sox (1951), and San Francisco Seals (1950) and New York Yankees (1955)—and one did so the same year, the Hollywood Stars and Chicago White Sox (1951).[3] The process of integration illustrated the need of the Major League teams to have relationships with integrated Minor League teams to develop and bring up players of color. Although many of the players coming into the Majors had professional experience in the Negro Leagues, organized baseball preferred that they moved into the Minors before playing for a Major League team. Some of the players who integrated a Minor League team would reap the benefit of the Major-Minor League affiliation and move up to achieve their dream of playing in Major League Baseball. Others found their careers limited to the Minors, but the players were still part of the movement for social change in American society.

The 1949 season marked the second season of integration for the San Diego Padres. In 1949 John Ritchey was no longer the lone nonwhite player on the San Diego Padres or in the PCL. With the start of the 1949 season three new teammates of color joined John Ritchey on the San Diego Padres' roster: Luke Easter (on March 30), Artie Wilson (on March 30), and Minnie Miñoso (on May 20). In 1949 the San Diego Padres and the Cleveland Indians affiliated. Cleveland Indians owner Bill Veeck sent Easter, Wilson, and Miñoso, all under contract with Cleveland, to San Diego. Despite the players' years of experience in the Negro Leagues, Veeck first sent each player to the Minors before including them on the Major League roster.

Luscious "Luke" Easter, a darker-skinned, Missouri-born left-handed hitter, became an immediate hitting sensation. Veeck had recommended Easter from the Negro League Homestead Grays to the Padres to fill their need for a right-handed hitter. Easter, however, was left-handed.[4] Born August 4, 1915, in St. Louis, Missouri, Luke Easter played first base. He first played professional baseball for the Titanium Giants in St. Louis in 1937. In 1942 he was drafted into the army. Easter received a medical discharge in 1943. In 1947 he joined the Homestead Grays after a year of barnstorming with the Cincinnati Crescents. In 1949 the Cleveland Indians, the second Major League team to integrate in 1947, signed Easter to a contract on February 19, 1949. The thirty-three-year-old Easter went to spring training with

Cleveland's Triple-A Minor League team, the Padres. Easter played eighty games with the Padres, playing in a series in San Francisco, Oakland, Los Angeles, and Hollywood, before Cleveland called him up.[5] On May 22, 1949, with Luke Easter on the San Diego Padres' roster, a new attendance record was set at Seals Stadium in San Francisco. The crowd of 23,366 included an estimated 8,000 blacks.[6] Easter batted .363, with 92 runs and 25 home runs in eighty games for the Padres, while playing with a broken kneecap.[7] Luke Easter made his Major League debut with the Cleveland Indians on August 11, 1949. He would play six seasons in Cleveland.

Like Easter, Artie Wilson had Negro League experience when he joined the San Diego Padres. Arthur Lee "Artie" Wilson was born on October 28, 1920, in Springfield, Alabama. Growing up in Birmingham, labeled during the Depression as the "worst hit town in the country,"[8] Wilson attended Tarrant City Elementary and Hooper City High School. He learned to play baseball first with a rubber ball and broomstick and then with a thread-wrapped golf ball. At the age of sixteen, Wilson divided his time between attending school and working at the American Cast Iron and Pipe Company (ACIPCO).[9] Artie Wilson played baseball in the industrial league of Birmingham for a team sponsored by his employer. The city's industrial league initially included thirty teams, including two white teams from ACIPCO. In 1929 the Colored YMCA organized the first Colored Industrial Baseball League, which included teams from eight companies, including the one from ACIPCO. A black pitcher recalled that the company supplied equal transportation and equipment for both the white and the black teams.[10] When he was eighteen, Wilson lost the top joint of his right thumb while working in the factory.[11] The injury never affected his ability to play baseball. In 1944 Wilson signed with the Birmingham Black Barons of the Negro National League.[12] As a shortstop for the Barons, Wilson's Negro League career lasted from 1944 to 1948. As the leadoff hitter in the lineup, Wilson won the batting title in 1947 and 1948. In 1948 his batting average was .402, above the rarely reached .400 average for hitters.[13] Wilson played in the Negro Leagues East-West All-Star Games for all but one of his years as a Black Baron.

Players who signed with the Pacific Coast League from the Negro Leagues sometimes faced contractual issues. The less formalized Negro Leagues could not always prove that they had a signed contract with a player. In 1947

Artie Wilson signed with the Cleveland Indians, and his contract became embroiled in controversy. According to the Commissioner's Office, in a memo dated May 13, 1949,[14] Wilson was under contract with the Birmingham Black Barons in 1948. In January 1949 the New York Yankees scouted Wilson and offered to purchase his contract from Tom Hayes, the Barons' president. The Yankees believed that Wilson agreed to a contract to play at the Triple-A level for $500 a month.[15] With the agreement the Yankees planned to send Wilson to the Yankees' Triple-A affiliate the Newark Bears in Newark, New Jersey. After agreeing to the contract with the Yankees, Hayes and Wilson reneged and entered into negotiations with Abe Saperstein, representative of the Cleveland Indians. Wilson signed a contract with Cleveland owner Bill Veeck. Mediation occurred after George Weiss, the general manager of the New York Yankees, challenged the Wilson-Cleveland contract by filing a grievance with the Commissioner's Office. Weiss charged Veeck with "unethical practices" for signing a player already under contract and filed a complaint on February 28, 1949.[16] Between February 28 and May 13, 1949, as the Commissioner's Office mediated the contract dispute, Cleveland sent Wilson to the San Diego Padres, with whom they had a working agreement.[17] On March 30, 1949, Ritchey, Easter, and Artie Wilson appeared on the San Diego roster to open the season. Wilson, the twenty-nine-year-old shortstop, had one hit in three at-bats in the seven-inning opener. On May 18, 1949, MLB commissioner Happy Chandler decided the New York–Cleveland contract dispute in favor of the Yankees, which would have sent Wilson to Newark, as stated in the original contract. However, the Yankees promptly sold Wilson's contract outright to the Oakland Oaks. Wilson never played in Newark but went from San Diego to Oakland two months into the season. His last game as a Padre was on May 15, 1949, and his first game as an Oak was May 22, 1949. Artie Wilson integrated the Oaks (as discussed below). The transition from the Negro Leagues to organized baseball was not without contractual problems for some players. As more and more players left the Negro Leagues for Major or Minor League teams, organized baseball had the upper hand in negotiations, as Negro League owners did not want to appear to oppose integration.

The third player of color signed by Cleveland Indians owner Bill Veeck for the 1949 season, Minnie Miñoso joined the Padres on May 24. The

Cuban-born Saturnino Orestes Armas "Minnie" Miñoso Arrieta began his multidecade professional baseball career in Cuba in 1945 and then played for the Negro League New York Cubans for three seasons, beginning in 1946. In 1948 Minnie Miñoso played eleven games with the Cleveland Indians' Single-A affiliate, the Dayton Indians, a team he integrated. While Miñoso was playing winter ball in Cuba between the 1948 and 1949 seasons, Hank Greenberg, the general manager of the Cleveland Indians, contacted him about returning to Dayton for the 1949 season. Through an interpreter Miñoso negotiated a new contract, which included an increase in his monthly salary from $700 to $1,000. Like other Latinos, Miñoso had to deal with the challenges of a different language and culture. Negotiating his contract with the Padres was difficult because "my language problem didn't exactly help me with my contract."[18] In 1949, after seven games with the Cleveland Indians, Miñoso returned to the Minor Leagues, joining John Ritchey, Luke Easter, and Artie Wilson on the San Diego Padres' roster.

In San Diego Miñoso gained professional experience in a more supportive environment. Cities in the Southwest, such as San Diego, could provide a Latino player support from the established Mexican American community.[19] In San Diego Miñoso found that the fans "were enthusiastic and 100 percent behind their team. Even though I had confidence in myself, the cheers and applause of the fans gave me more will and fortitude."[20] Miñoso had other teammates of color to support him. He and Luke Easter roomed together, although Miñoso claimed that the team management discouraged the association of the two men. "We'd travel around a lot after hours, and he really knew the streets. But management didn't approve of our association. Luke had a passion for women, and the owners felt he was a bad influence on me. I told Luke that the club didn't want me hanging around with him, and that I didn't know why. I think he was hurt, but said he understood."[21]

As Miñoso described, in San Diego and the other cities of PCL teams, he and Luke Easter might go out after the game. Miñoso does not describe social activity limited to certain areas of town or black-owned businesses. If the two players had felt limited in where they could travel, maybe the Padre management would have been less concerned with their activities. After another season with the Padres, Miñoso returned to the Majors, playing with the Cleveland Indians again before Bill Veeck traded him to the Chicago White Sox. Minnie Miñoso integrated the White Sox on May 5, 1951. He played seventeen seasons in the Major Leagues.

In 1948 John Ritchey was the only player of color on any roster in the PCL. During the 1949 season Ritchey had several teammates who were nonwhite. In May Ritchey and his teammates of color would also have black opponents.

Following the San Diego Padres, the Oakland Oaks became the second Pacific Coast League team to integrate. Artie Wilson spent almost two months with the San Diego Padres at the start of the 1949 season. After the settlement of his contractual issue sent him to Oakland, Wilson integrated the Oakland Oaks on May 22, 1949. In addition to new contractual obligations, players like Wilson faced new social realities while playing in the Pacific Coast League. In his case they were not all negative. While in Oakland, as the only African American player on the Oakland Oaks' roster, Artie Wilson expected to room by himself. However, teammate Billy Martin, the future brash New York Yankee player and manager, asked to be Artie Wilson's roommate. When Martin volunteered to be Wilson's roommate, they broke another barrier of segregation. Of Martin Wilson said, "He was a super guy."[22] Another black player joined Wilson on the Oaks that season. On July 13 Parnell "Perry" Woods joined the Oaks, giving all three integrated PCL teams more than one black player on the roster.[23]

The signing of players of color to contracts with the PCL included players who did not ever play during the regular season. Before the start of spring training in 1949, two players, Curtis Roberts and Gene Richardson, the latter a native of San Diego, both under contract with the Kansas City Monarchs of the Negro Leagues, had a one-day tryout with the Oaks in Emeryville Park. While the pair were scheduled to work out for a week, weather cut the workout to one day. Oaks manager Charlie Dressen evaluated Roberts and Richardson as not advanced enough for the Oaks, and he recommended not purchasing their contracts from the Monarchs. Oakland owner Brick Laws supported the decision of his new manager.[24] After returning from spring training and looking at Richardson again, the Oakland Oaks made a cash offer to the Kansas City Monarchs for the nineteen-year-old pitcher's contract, but Richardson would never play for the Oaks, nor would he ever play in organized baseball.[25] Curt Roberts would play in the Major

Leagues with the Pittsburgh Pirates. As integration took hold, Major and Minor League teams had their pick of the players from the Negro Leagues. They could offer tryouts or workouts to evaluate the players, but they were not obligated to sign them to contracts.

The experience of the players of color led PCL managers to have to develop different strategies of play. In 1949, the year Wilson won the PCL batting championship, his 211 hits forced San Francisco Seals manger Lefty O'Doul to institute a "reserve shift" that brought the center fielder in as shortstop and, with the exception of the first baseman, positioned all of the other fielders to the left of second base. This strategy did not prevent Artie Wilson from attaining hitting success. In 1951 the Major League New York Giants purchased Wilson's contract. Wilson hit .182 in twenty-two at bats in nineteen games with the Giants during the 1951 season. Midseason, the Giants optioned the thirty-year-old Wilson to the Ottawa Giants of the International League and then to the Minneapolis Millers of the American Association. Wilson returned to Oakland by the end of the summer. His return drew a large crowd, and he finished the season hitting .255 in eighty-one games. In 1952 Wilson's contract was sold to the PCL Seattle Rainiers. Artie Wilson played in only nineteen games at the Major League level, but had integration occurred early in his playing career, it certainly would have been longer.

In 1949 team rosters began to include dark-skinned Latino players in addition to African Americans. The Afro-Cuban Minnie Miñoso joined the San Diego Padres in 1949, and two Latino players, a Panamanian and a Cuban, integrated the Portland Beavers in 1949. Born May 22, 1922, in the Panama Canal Zone, Frank Samuel Austin was a Panamanian infielder with speed. In 1944 the twenty-two-year-old Austin signed with the Philadelphia Stars of the Negro National League. For five seasons Austin worked the infield for the Stars as a shortstop. Austin's teammate Marvin Williams moved from shortstop to second base because Austin could play only as a shortstop.[26] Mahlon Duckett and Austin produced one of the best double-play combinations in baseball, and Duckett recalled Austin as one of the best shortstops with whom he played.[27] In 1945 Austin participated in his first of six East-West All-Star Games. He also played winter ball in Venezuela and Panama. Austin, like other Negro League players, was able to move across the boundaries of the United States and Latin America, playing baseball where he could. Playing on mixed teams of whites, blacks, and Latinos, players of color showed that integration could be successful.[28] The players carried that experience with them as they played on integrated teams in the United States.

Luis Márquez joined Frank Austin on the Portland Beavers' roster in May 1949. Born October 25, 1925, in Aguadilla, Puerto Rico, Márquez played in both the infield and the outfield and had incredible speed on the bases. Márquez competed in track in high school. His baseball career began with the Aguadilla-Mayaguez Indians of Puerto Rico.[29] In 1945 Luis Márquez joined the New York Black Yankees. His Negro League career also included time as a Homestead Gray and as a Baltimore Elite Giant. In February 1949 the New York Yankees signed Márquez. The Homestead Grays and the Baltimore Elite Giants both felt they had the right to negotiate a Major League contract for Márquez. The Grays signed a contract with the Cleveland Indians, and the Giants signed with the New York Yankees. In May 1949 the Commissioner's Office awarded Márquez's contract to the Cleveland Indians, who then optioned Márquez to Portland at the same time the Yankees sold Frank Austin's contract to the Beavers.[30]

Frank Austin never played Major League Baseball, but the Yankees signed him in 1949 to fill the place of Artie Wilson after the contract dispute between Wilson and the Yankees. The Yankees requested that the Commissioner's Office investigate the disputes with the contracts of Artie Wilson and Luis Márquez. During the investigation Wilson remained in the Cleveland organization and Márquez as a Yankee. The Yankees signed Austin on February 26, 1949. He played nineteen games with the Yankees' Triple-A affiliate the Newark Bears. Márquez went to Newark with Austin, playing in eighteen games, and then on to Portland, Oregon.

With the arrival of Austin and Márquez in Portland in May 1949, the Portland Beavers became the third PCL team to integrate. The headline on Monday morning in the *Portland Oregonian* read, "Portland to Get 2 Negro Players." The article that followed began, "In a surprise strengthening move the Portland Beavers added to their roster two new colored players; the first in Vaughn Street home history, one by outright purchase and the other on option."[31] The article stated that general manager Bill Mulligan had previously considered Austin, and he signed Márquez to provide Austin with a roommate. As previously noted, it was common in the integration process for teams to sign players of color to teams two at a time so they would have a roommate. If they did not have a roommate, they frequently roomed alone. Austin also served as translator for Márquez, who did not speak English.[32]

Frank Austin played his first game as a shortstop for the Portland Beavers team on Tuesday, May 24, 1949, in Hollywood. He had one hit in four at bats. On Friday, May 27, Márquez arrived from New York by plane at noon and played in the outfield the same day, in the fourth game of the series, going 0 for 4.[33] On July 23, 1949, Art Pennington, an outfielder who played in the Negro Leagues and the Mexican Leagues, joined Austin and Márquez on the Beavers for twenty games. Having three players of color on one team at one time came second only to San Diego in 1949, who had four on their roster. On May 30, 1949, when the Portland Beavers played in San Diego, it was the first time opposing teams in the PCL each had players of color in their lineups.

In many ways the careers of Frank Austin and Luis Márquez appear like those of other players who came from the Negro Leagues into organized baseball after World War II. Austin and Márquez, however, represent racial and cultural diversity that the management of PCL did not comprehend. The city saw the two players as "the first Negroes ever to wear Beaver garb."[34] This categorization of African American overlooks their Latin heritage and culture. Players who spoke Spanish, as Márquez did, did not receive support from the team, such as translators, but instead relied on teammates. Except for the notation that the two were the first blacks to play in Portland, the papers do not make an issue of their race. There are no comments about the players from the management or other players. Baseball history links Frank Austin and Luis Márquez on May 22, 1949, but other than sharing the same debut date, the two did not seem to share much else. Their diverging careers not only demonstrate that integration was more than black and white but illustrate the multiplicity of the Latino experience as well.

Minnie Miñoso, Frank Austin, and Luis Márquez were not the first Latinos to play professional baseball. Between 1882 and 1947 fifty-three Latino players played for a dozen different teams. Mostly Cuban, some of the players came from places in the Caribbean, such as Puerto Rico, or South American countries such as Colombia and Venezuela. Lighter skinned, frequently from wealthy families, and often educated in the United States,[35] these players focused on their Spanish heritage to identify themselves as "not black." By emphasizing ancestry from Spain, a European country, these Latinos found a level of acceptance in the United States and on the baseball diamond.

Afro-Latinos did not receive opportunities in either Major League Baseball or the leagues in Cuba before Jackie Robinson began the process of integration in organized baseball. Professional baseball and American society judged these players not by their countries of origin but by their skin color. The Negro Leagues welcomed dark-skinned Latino players that Major or Minor Leagues denied. Afro-Latino players faced more than the racism of baseball and American society. Those who were foreign born and Spanish speakers also had to contend with cultural adjustments. Players who did not understand English well enough to order a meal in a restaurant either learned how to order one entrée and ate it every time they went out or would order the same thing as a teammate. If he spoke Spanish, a dark-skinned Latino might receive different treatment from the American-born blacks. Father of Hall of Famer Orlando Cepeda, Puerto Rican Pedro, or Perucho, Cepeda chose not to play in the United States for fear he would face segregation with his dark skin.[36] For some the chance to play Negro League baseball was not enough to suffer the social injustices of the United States.

Of the thirty-one players with African ancestry who played in the PCL between 1948 and 1952, five were foreign born (two in Cuba, two in Panama, and one in Puerto Rico). Fourteen of them played during the summer months in Latin American leagues, with most playing in the Mexican Leagues. Twenty-five of them spent time playing winter ball in Latin American leagues, with most of the players going to Puerto Rico. Fifteen of the thirty-one players went on to play in the Major Leagues. Sixteen African American and Latino players from PCL teams during the postintegration period (1953–57) also played in Latin America. Time in the Latin leagues gave black players a chance to experience a less segregated society, gain playing time against professional white players, and develop their baseball skills.[37]

Both the United States and Cuba influenced the development of the game across Mexico. Negro League third baseman Ray Dandridge, who would play for the Oakland Oaks and Sacramento Solons of the PCL in 1953, left his $150 monthly salary with the Newark Eagles for a $500 monthly salary in Mexico in 1940. He liked Mexico so much he played there nine seasons. Dandridge's daughter Delores had happy memories of growing up in Mexico City. "We had a wonderful childhood while my father played ball there." Jorge Pasquel played an important role in expanding the Mexican Leagues and bringing in African Americans in the 1940s and 1950s. For his players, such as Ray Dandridge, Pasquel would provide housing allowances, tutors, and maids. Pasquel and the other owners offered a life the players could not have in the United States. Monte Irvin remembered Jorge Pasquel: "He treated us like human beings. He didn't think he was superior. He was fair minded. Color didn't mean anything to him. If he liked you, he'd do anything for you."[38]

After World War II, as the Mexican Leagues increased their recruitment of white players from the United States, their rosters became a mixture of black, white, and Latin players from both sides of the border. As white Major Leaguers traveled to Mexico to find the same opportunities blacks had found since the 1930s, black players faced discrimination from those whites. Mexican fans accepted African Americans in a way that was not true for white players. Black players learned Spanish when many of the white players did not. World travels across Latin America had made many of the African American players more sophisticated than their white counterparts who came from small rural communities.[39] Black players in Mexico had other African American teammates with whom they could bond. When they integrated Major League Baseball, they signed to a team one or two at a time. Playing integrated games without racial problems proved that a black catcher could catch for a white pitcher or a black coach could advise a white player without racial incident. These players would then return to the United States and maybe be more accepting as integration came to the Minor and Major Leagues.

The only racial difficulties players had in Mexico were with white tourists from the United States. When a hotel owner changed his policy of letting African Americans stay there to accommodate the white tourists from the United States who complained about staying in the same hotel as an African American, Pasquel found the player his own apartment, separate from the rest of the team. With a few exceptions most Mexicans had not seen black people before the African American ballplayers arrived. Mexicans welcomed and accepted the foreign players. Art Pennington married a Mexican woman.

When they rode the train home to Little Rock, Arkansas, his wife was asked to move to the white section of the train, but Pennington refused to let her. In Little Rock Pennington and his wife had to wait in their respective waiting rooms until his parents arrived to take them home.[40] In Mexico they traveled together as a married couple. In the South their status changed to a black man traveling with a white woman. Even though the players returned to the United States to live again in a separate but not equal world, their time in Mexico and other Latin countries must have given them a break from living the double consciousness that W. E. B. DuBois described and provided a few weeks or months of living like men.

Many of the players in the Negro Leagues played during the off-season in various countries across Latin America. The Cuban Winter League (from 1947), Panamanian Winter League (from 1948), Puerto Rican Winter League (from 1948), Venezuelan Winter League (from 1948), Dominican Winter League (from 1955), and Nicaraguan Winter League (from 1955) offered professional baseball players the opportunity to play during the winter months when Major and Minor League Baseball in the United States was not in season.[41] From a professional skill perspective, winter baseball allowed players to play almost year-round. During the winter of 1948–49, John Ritchey, the first African American in the PCL, played in Caracas, Venezuela, with a batting average of .350. He said he learned how to hit left-handed pitchers, one of his weaknesses from the previous year. He told a San Diego newspaper, "There aren't many good ball players in Venezuela, but they are good instructors."[42] Playing over the winter months and receiving suggestions from various coaches improved Ritchey's game. That improvement would assist in his successes during the regular season. The African American players who integrated had to be better than average to sign contracts in the Major or Minor Leagues.

Before the 1949 season Ritchey's older brother Bert reported to the newspaper that younger brother Johnny would arrive home on February 20 and then report to Ontario, California, for the Padres' spring training. Going immediately from winter ball to spring training meant that Ritchey would already be in shape for the Padres' season. An interviewer said to Ritchey, "You must be in love with this game of baseball to play it all year round." Ritchey responded, "I just wish I loved it twice as much as I do."[43]

Playing during the winter did not require traveling to South America. Over the 1950–51 winter season each weekend Ritchey would drive seven hundred miles south from San Diego to play in the Mexican Leagues. This additional practice made the players better and gave them more chances for success in the United States.

Another factor that helped players like Ritchey succeed in Venezuela and other places was that he traveled with his wife, Lydia, and seven-month-old daughter, Johana. "The baby stood the plane trip better than my wife and I. She's a great girl. . . . We go everywhere we can together. We had a swell time in Venezuela even though they did have a revolution and the cost of living was sky high."[44] That the Ritcheys could travel as a family could only help Ritchey in focusing on the job he had to do. Having his family with him could also help with the cultural adjustments of being in South America. In another interview several years later when asked about life in Venezuela, Ritchey remarked, "[The] only thing is, they don't eat vegetables in Venezuela! Now, how can anyone be at home without eating vegetables at mealtimes? The wife and I bought a whole case of baby vegetables in cans when we sailed from New York, just in case they didn't sell it down there. . . . [W]hen we kept getting that starchy food thrown at us one time after another, we wound up eating the youngster's food."[45] In the United States married players usually did not travel with the families during the season. In the off-season Ritchey could bring his entire family with him.

Playing in the Winter Leagues, African Americans faced more than just cultural differences. Second to the United States, African Americans found segregation and racism in Cuba. Cubans adopted the sport very quickly in the nineteenth century. Baseball continued to grow after the Spanish-American War. During the first two decades of the twentieth century, white Major Leaguers toured Cuba. They played on teams with Cuban players but not Afro-Cubans. The segregation of the United States found its way onto the Cuban baseball diamond as well. The 1930s, '40s, and '50s were the best time for winter baseball in Cuba. Cuban-born Minnie Miñoso played for Marianao in the Cuban Winter League in 1944. Jorge Pasquel tried to persuade him to play in Mexico with $30,000 for two years and racial equality. Miñoso wanted to play in the United States. He countered that while he had not yet been to the United States to experience society there, he was used to racial discrimination in Cuba. Miñoso said, "In Cuba, it was much the same, but the sign said Private. That's the key difference. They made them private clubs that people could not get into."[46] After two years with the San Diego Padres in 1949 and 1950, Miñoso made it to the Major Leagues. After a fifteen-year Major League career, he spent five seasons in Mexico.

In the U.S. territory of Puerto Rico the racial situation for black players was not much better than in Cuba. Following the Cuban model, a winter league developed in the 1930s. Monte Irvin recalled of the 1941–42 season, "We had a rough time in Puerto Rico. Sometimes it was worse than the United States."[47] Not all cities and countries welcomed black players, but most found the segregation less than in the United States and that the benefits outweighed the costs.

The process of integrating professional baseball in the United States required many elements for success. The experience of African American PCL players in Latin American leagues was an important part of that process. African Americans had to be better players than their white counterparts to succeed as professional baseball players. Playing in the Latin leagues was one way to become a better player. In most cases black players could leave behind the segregation of the United States and live as equals in Latin American countries. They brought their social, cultural, and baseball experiences home to the United States to face the challenge of integrating America's pastime.

The cities of the Pacific Coast League team offered a different experience for players of color. As Samuel Regalado argued, "In the American West, the process of acculturating the Latin American player appeared much easier."[48] Latin players like Minnie Miñoso could find support in western cities, especially those with Spanish-speaking populations. In the Southwest, but particularly in Los Angeles, Mexicans and Mexican Americans played on baseball teams in school, in college, and as adults.[49] A reporter for the Nicaraguan newspaper *La Prensa* noticed that prior to Latino players joining PCL teams, the local Spanish-speaking fans did not follow the PCL.[50] These fans supported the Latino players as they joined PCL teams.

Light-skinned Latinos began playing in the Pacific Coast League before John Ritchey integrated the Padres in 1948. Like in the Major Leagues, the PCL teams included light-skinned Latinos. Those players with lighter skin did not face the same kind or racism in the United States as those with darker skin. Mexico-born Jesse Flores played for the Los Angeles Angels from 1939 to 1942 and was a Padre teammate of John Ritchey in 1948 and 1949. His career included twelve seasons in the Minors and seven in Major League Baseball. Born in Wilmington, California, Froilan "Nanny" Fernandez played eight seasons in the PCL before and after his time in the Majors. In 1944 San Diego–born Manuel P. "Nay" Hernandez played thirty games with the Padres.[51] Mexican-born José Bache played in the Mexican Leagues before joining the San Diego Padres in 1951. Jose Guillermo Santiago played for the Padres the same season. *The PCL Sketchbook* for 1951 lists Manuel Ruiz Perez as a Mexico-born pitcher from El Paso. His PCL career began in Hollywood in 1942 and continued with San Francisco. Manuel Echeveria played in three games for the San Diego Padres in 1951. Venezuelan-born Alejandro "Álex" Carrasquel played in the Majors with the Washington Senators before joining the Sacramento Solons in 1951. Mexico-born Guillermo Romero "Memo" Luna played ten seasons in the Minors and pitched one game for the St. Louis Cardinals in 1954. His time in the PCL included two seasons in San Diego, in 1952 and 1953. Luna was a popular pitcher, especially with Mexican and Mexican American fans. Throughout California Mexican American fans honored Memo Luna at ceremonies within their communities.[52]

Professional baseball teams excluded dark-skinned Latinos during the period of segregation. Their ability to join a team depended not on their place of birth but on their skin color. During integration the signing of African American players also opened doors for dark-skinned Latinos. Other dark-skinned Latinos soon joined Minnie Miñoso, Frank Austin, and Luis Márquez on PCL rosters. Rafael Miguel "Ray" Noble, an Afro-Cuban catcher, played for Oakland in 1950. He played thirteen seasons in the Minor Leagues, two for the PCL, and parts of three seasons in the Majors. In 1951 Raul Lopez pitched and lost two games for the Oakland Oaks. The Cuban-born Lopez would play four seasons in the Minors. Cuban-born Lorenzo Cabrera played two years in the Negro Leagues before joining the Oakland Oaks in 1951.

After the years of integration three other Latino players appeared on PCL rosters. The dark-skinned, Cuban-born Lino Doñoso played for Hollywood from 1954 to 1956, and Cuban-born René Valdés played for Portland in 1956. Rudy Regalado played in the PCL from 1957 to 1960 with the San Diego Padres and the Seattle Rainiers. Most Americans looked through a racial rather than an ethnic or cultural lens to see skin color. Many Americans would prejudge a dark-skinned player like Minnie Miñoso to be African American rather than Afro-Latino. Lighter-skinned Latino players from Mexico, the Caribbean, or Latin America did not face the same discrimination as did those whose skin was darker. Integration opened up opportunities for dark-skinned players to join their lighter-skinned Latino teammates.

Some of the players who integrated the PCL and other teams in organized baseball had experience in the Mexican Leagues in addition to their time in the Negro Leagues. Before he came to the Pacific Coast League, African American Booker McDaniels had a career as a pitcher with the Kansas City Monarchs. He also played in Veracruz, San Luis, and Mexico City, Mexico, before he joined the Los Angeles Angels. Born in 1912, in Blackwell, Arkansas, McDaniels and his three brothers grew up in nearby Morrilton, essentially raising themselves after their mother died.[53] McDaniels grew up playing baseball and, in 1940, signed with the Kansas City Monarchs of the Negro National League. The right-handed pitcher played for the Monarchs for the next five seasons. Nicknamed "Cannonball," McDaniels "could throw harder than four claps of thunder."[54] From 1941 to 1943 he had twenty-one wins and only one loss. Monarch's teammate and future Hall of Famer Satchel Paige frequently overshadowed McDaniels, but McDaniels was one of the "Big Four" in the pitching rotation. In 1945 he made his only appearance in the Negro Leagues East-West All-Star Game. McDaniels received a physical deferment and continued playing baseball through World War II.[55]

During the 1940s the Negro Leagues faced competition from the Mexican Leagues. In 1946 McDaniels became one in the tide of players traveling south to play in Mexican Leagues. The following year he was one of twenty-six players from the Negro Leagues who went to Mexico to play. Through the 1930s and 1940s team owners such as Mexican millionaire Jorge Pasquel raided the Negro Leagues for talent to bring to Mexico. Many of the Negro League players who traveled to Mexico and other Latin American countries spoke no Spanish and had to adjust to life in a foreign country. Ballplayers went to Latin American countries to stay in shape during the winter season and to earn extra money. Americans could earn a good salary and frequently had better accommodations while traveling and played in higher-quality stadiums than they had in the Negro Leagues. Lighter-skinned blacks could find better treatment than in America, but darker-skinned players still faced discrimination.[56] Individuals who went to Mexico faced a five-year ban from playing in the Negro Leagues, an effort to prevent players from abandoning their Negro League contracts. On February 26, 1949, the *Chicago Defender* reported that the Negro American League had reinstated McDaniels and that he would return to the Kansas City Monarchs.[57] While he thought he was returning to the Negro Leagues, Booker McDaniels instead had the chance to play in organized baseball. McDaniels returned to the Kansas City Monarchs for the start of the 1949 season, but on June 14 the Chicago Cubs organization purchased McDaniels's contract for $7,500.[58] Effa Manley, co-owner of the Negro Leagues' Newark Eagles, received only $5,000 for Larry Doby's contract when he joined the Cleveland Indians in 1947. By 1949, when the Major and Minor League rosters opened to black players, the compensation the Negro League teams received was more appropriate to the value of their contracts. The Negro League teams began to recoup money for the contracts of the players going into the Minor and Major Leagues.

The Cubs sent Booker McDaniels to their Pacific Coast League affiliate, the Los Angeles Angels. On June 15, 1949, McDaniels pitched in his first game as an Angel against Portland. He won the game 8–3, allowing five hits. The *Los Angeles Times* noted that McDaniels's appearance marked the first time an African American pitcher played in the Pacific Coast League: "McDaniels's chore on the mound represented the first time a Negro pitcher had performed in the league and he made good."[59] McDaniels's second game was June 21 and his third five days later. The Angels won each game. The notation that a player of color was making history was rarely more than one line in the report of the game. In every report of his first three games, the paper notes that McDaniels was the first "Negro" pitcher. John Ritchey and Artie Wilson did not receive the same kind of notation after their first games. The Los Angeles Angels released Booker McDaniels in 1950. With the integration of the San Diego Padres, Oakland Oaks, Portland Beavers, and Los Angeles Angels, the Pacific Coast League had integrated half of its eight teams in just three seasons.

The continued signing of players of color by the San Diego Padres and the successful integration of three additional teams in the Pacific Coast League during the 1949 season show integration as a process gaining momentum but still facing challenges. Moving beyond the signing of one player to one team, integration brought eleven different players onto team rosters in 1949. The players, who included dark-skinned Latinos, brought their professional experience and cultural diversity to the league. Although players faced discrimination and racism on and off the field, they also found support from the team and the fans when they helped win games. The PCL was one of eighteen different Minor Leagues across the country that shifted from segregated to integrated teams.

1. Jimmy Claxton played for the Oakland Oaks in 1916. His baseball career spanned four decades. Courtesy of the Shanaman Sports Museum, Tacoma, Washington.

2. *(above)* Kenso Nushida pitched for the Sacramento Senators in 1932. Mark Macrae Collection.

3. *(right)* Lee Gum Hong pitched for the Oakland Oaks in 1932. Mark Macrae Collection.

4. San Diego Padres owner Bill Starr and John Ritchey shake hands outside of the San Diego Padres' offices. National Baseball Hall of Fame and Museum, Cooperstown, New York.

5. John Ritchey integrated the San Diego Padres and the Pacific Coast League on March 30, 1948. Mark Macrae Collection.

6. Artie Wilson integrated the Oakland Oaks on May 22, 1949. Mark Macrae Collection.

7. Frank Austin integrated the Portland Beavers on May 24, 1949. Mark Macrae Collection.

8. (*left*) With Frank Austin, Luis Márquez joined the roster of the Portland Beavers on May 24, 1949. Mark Macrae Collection.

9. (*above*) Booker McDaniels integrated the Los Angeles Angels on June 15, 1949. Dave Eskenazi Collection.

10. Marvin Williams integrated the Sacramento Solons on August 27, 1950. He played with the Seattle Rainiers in 1955. Mark Macrae Collection.

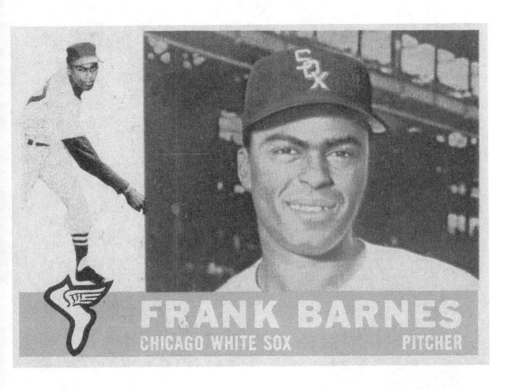

11. Frank Barnes integrated the San Francisco Seals on March 31, 1951. On May 19, 1960, he joined the Chicago White Sox. Topps® trading card used courtesy of the Topps Company, Inc.

12. Roy Welmaker integrated the Hollywood Stars on May 11, 1951. He also played for the Portland Beavers in 1952 and 1953. Dave Eskenazi Collection.

13. Bob Boyd integrated the Seattle Rainiers on April 1, 1952. Dave Eskenazi Collection.

14. With Bob Boyd, Artie Wilson first played for the Seattle Rainiers on April 1, 1952. He celebrates in the locker room with Seattle Rainiers teammates Merl Combs, Gordon Goldsberry, Clarence Maddern, and Bill Evans in 1953. Dave Eskenazi Collection.

CHAPTER 5

THE PACIFIC COAST LEAGUE
INTEGRATES, 1950–52

I've never had bad feelings toward anybody; I was just glad to be able to play when I did.

Artie Wilson, quoted in Eric Enders, "The Last .400 Hitter"

On October 31, 2010, the man who hit .400 with the Birmingham Black Barons in 1948 passed away in Portland, Oregon. Artie Wilson, born in Jefferson County, Alabama, had journeyed through ninety years, many of which were spent on the baseball diamond. Although he struggled with Alzheimer's at the end of his life, he could still root for his favorite team, the San Francisco Giants. In 1951 he played nineteen games with the New York Giants, but his baseball career included five seasons in the Negro Leagues and ten in the Minors. When he arrived in San Diego in 1949, Artie Wilson joined a team that John Ritchey had already integrated. Moving to Oakland, Wilson integrated that team and, with Bob Boyd, would integrate the Seattle Rainiers in 1952. Artie Wilson would play for six of the eight teams of the PCL and would end his professional baseball career with Portland in 1962. Wilson was only one of two players not born in the West who would choose to live there for the rest of his life. Artie Wilson's career took him from the Negro Leagues to the Minor League to the Major League and back to the Minors. His career bridged segregation and integration. Although he may not have had the Major League career he could only dream of as a child in Alabama, Wilson played an important role in integrating the Pacific Coast League. Artie Wilson's career, which included playing for multiple teams in various leagues, exemplifies the reality of many of those who played during the period of integration.

After the first team of the Pacific Coast League integrated, it took only five seasons for the remaining seven teams to add players of color to their rosters. The PCL integrated at a faster pace than the Major Leagues, which did not integrate all sixteen of its teams until 1959. By August 1950, in their third season of integration, 60 percent of the PCL teams had signed at least one player of color, whereas the Major League, in its fourth year of integration, had players of color on 25 percent of their sixteen teams. In 1951 the PCL teams fielded more black players than any other Minor League.[1] The Pacific Coast League was the first league to integrate all of its teams. During the 1950, 1951, and 1952 seasons the Sacramento Solons, the San Francisco Seals, the Hollywood Stars, and the Seattle Rainiers each added players of color to their rosters. The integration of all eight PCL teams in just five years shows that the process had not only gained momentum but, by reaching all of the teams, become part of a social movement for change in the West.

Major League Baseball continued its slow pace of integrating teams in the 1950s. Sam Jethroe became a Boston Brave on April 18, 1950. His Negro League career began twelve years earlier in Indianapolis. Jethroe played in the International League, the American Association, and the National League before ending his career with the Toronto Maple Leafs in 1958. The Braves were the only Major League team to integrate in 1950. On April 30, 1951, Minnie Miñoso became a Chicago White Sox as part of a three-team trade. A San Diego Padre in 1949, Miñoso had played five seasons in the Negro Leagues and for the Single-A Dayton Indians before bouncing between the San Diego Padres and the Cleveland Indians from 1949 to 1951. His arrival in Chicago on May 5, 1951, marked the sixth Major League team to integrate in six seasons. No Major League team would integrate in 1952. When the Pacific Coast League had added players of color to all eight of its teams at the start of the 1952 season, only six of the sixteen Major Leagues teams had integrated.

In contrast to the Major Leagues, the Minor Leagues integrated more quickly in the 1950s. The 1950 season saw six new Minor Leagues integrate, and 1951 included two more. During the 1952 season the integration of Minor Leagues reached a peak. With an additional ten leagues adding integrated teams, and new teams integrating within leagues that already had teams with players of color, the process of integration reached across the country, including into leagues in southern states.

The thirty-one players of color who played on the eight teams of the PCL from 1948 to 1952 already had a variety of professional baseball experience when they joined PCL teams.[2] Their experience included Negro Leagues, Mexican Leagues, and playing winter ball in California, the Caribbean, or Latin America. Twenty-eight of the thirty-one players had experience in the Negro Leagues. The shortest time in the Negro Leagues was 1 season, the longest 13. Parnell Woods played 13 seasons in the Negro Leagues before playing forty games with the Oakland Oaks. The average time in the Negro Leagues for those players was 5.35 seasons.

Fourteen of the thirty-one players had spent time playing in Latin America, and nineteen played winter baseball before, during, or after their time in the PCL. Once they made it to the Pacific Coast League, the players of color averaged 2.77 seasons. The shortest time in the PCL was one game, while the longest tenure was 9 seasons. Of the thirty-one players, fifteen would play in Major League Baseball. The first to move up to the Majors from the PCL would do so in 1949. The last would go to the Majors in 1955. Jay Heard had the shortest Major League career, playing two games with the Baltimore Orioles, and Minnie Miñoso had the longest, playing in 17 different seasons, in Cleveland, Chicago, Washington, and St. Louis.

Two players of color from the PCL would integrate two Major League teams, Miñoso with the Chicago White Sox in 1951 and Tom Alston, the first African American to play for the St. Louis Cardinals, in 1954. None of the players who played in the PCL between 1948 and 1952 would be elected to the Baseball Hall of Fame, but Hall of Famers Ray Dandridge, Larry Doby, and Monte Irvin played in the PCL after 1952. Five of the integrating players served in the military, during either World War II or Korea, but all served before their baseball careers.

With most having already played multiple seasons in the Negro Leagues, the thirty-one players who would move from the Negro Leagues to Minor and Major League teams had varying lengths to their careers in organized baseball. For many, it depended on their age at the time of integration. The players who played in organized baseball proved that, when given the chance, those whom organized baseball had excluded for more than seventy years were players of equal, and sometimes better, quality. Once professional baseball opened the doors to all races, the teams and leagues saw short- and long-term benefits.

Despite their previous professional experience, those players who integrated teams faced racism on and off the field. Artie Wilson, who integrated the Oakland Oaks in 1951, recalled that a white player on the team refused to play with blacks and left the team.[3] Wilson also remembered a heckler who specifically targeted him each time he played in Sacramento.[4] Negro League veteran Lorenzo "Piper" Davis, who also became an Oakland Oak in 1951, noted that racist fans called him "quite a few names" from the stands. "One guy was hollering 'Stick (the ball) in that nigger's ear.' . . . I hit a home run and went over to him and said, 'Take that!' He didn't say anything."[5]

The treatment of players by the team management varied by team. Dorothy Thurman, the wife of Bob Thurman, who played for the San Francisco Seals in 1951, recalled, "They (management) wanted to use Bob for a workhorse. . . . They weren't concerned about (his) career or whether he advanced beyond that. They felt he should be grateful for playing with white players."[6] When Piper Davis played for the Oakland Oaks in 1951, the team hotel refused to book a room for him when the team no longer paid for player housing. The hotel staff said they could no longer accommodate him. Life on the road could be very lonely for those players who were the only player of color on a team. Bob Thurman recalled, "I played on four different Triple A teams by myself, and that was rough. . . . I would go to the movies by myself. . . . If you had a bad day, you didn't have anybody to talk to. You'd talk to yourself. . . . You had to be like a steel man to take being alone."[7] Even though they already had years of professional experience, players of color would take the opportunity to play at the Minor League level even if they were overqualified because it might lead to the chance to play at the Major League level. They were willing to put up with racism and discrimination, and sometimes endure physical injury, to have that possibility.

Pitchers of the opposing teams would sometimes target the players of color and purposely throw beanballs. Since the injuries happened all across the PCL, it was not isolated to one or two teams. In 1949 injuries hospitalized one in four black nonpitchers playing in leagues at the Triple-A level. On July 26, 1949, an opposing pitcher knocked Parnell Woods unconscious with a pitch, and Woods was carried off the field on a stretcher.[8] In 1949 Luke Easter had so many pitches thrown at him that PCL president Clarence Rowland issued a memorandum against the use of the beanball.[9] During the first game of the 1951 season Portland Beaver Frank Austin was hit with a pitch. Six weeks into the season Sacramento Solons first baseman Bob Boyd went to the hospital for X-rays after a pitch hit him in the head.[10] In 1952 white San Francisco Seals pitcher Bill Boemler threw at Piper Davis and catcher Ray Noble, both black players. On July 27, after Boemler's pitches knocked Davis to the ground twice, Davis forcefully ran into Boemler as he headed into home two batters later. Tagged out by the pitcher, Davis began a fight with Boemler, and the benches of each team emptied to create "one of the biggest brawls ever seen in the Oakland ball park."[11] While the *Los Angeles Times* does not reference race as a cause of the fight, Davis remembered that "Noble was hitting everything white that was coming toward him."[12] It was common for pitchers in the PCL or at any level, including the Major Leagues,[13] to hit players of color purposely with pitches more often than whites. Since it was accepted practice in the Majors, it reasons that it was also accepted in the Minors.

Managers of baseball teams appeared to have a say in maintaining the status quo of segregation or forward progress with integration. Oakland Oaks manager Johnny Vergez appeared to stop Oaks Owner Vic Devincenzi from allowing a tryout of Chet Brewer and Lou Dials in April 1943. Once the process of integration began, the managers of the teams had differing responses. With the exception of San Francisco Seals manager Lefty O'Doul, the eight men who managed PCL teams in the year each team integrated did not leave documentation of their views on the subject of integration one way or another.

Of the racial views held by the twenty-seven men who managed PCL teams between the 1948 and 1952 seasons, records are still slim, but the black press did publish articles about the racial opinions of some of them. In December 1948 the *Los Angeles Sentinel* reported that Bucky Harris would manage the San Diego Padres in 1949. "Harris, a long-time manager of the Washington Senators, has had no experience with Negro players. However, he is a native of Pennsylvania, is rated a 'nice guy' and probably will go along with the program."[14] Since the 1949 roster of the San Diego Padres included four black players, it does appear that Bucky Harris either supported integration or, at least, did not obstruct it. That year Harris was critical of Artie Wilson's contributions to the team. When Wilson left San Diego to join the roster to the Oakland Oaks in May 1949, Wilson found a supportive manager in Charlie Dressen. "Dressen literally welcomed him with open arms. . . . On numerous mornings and afternoons, Dressen worked with Wilson to improve his fielding, throwing and correcting his hitting."[15] Whether Dressen supported integration or not, he did support his player who was African American and provided extra attention to improve his skills. In 1950 the *Chicago Defender* accused Hollywood Stars manager Fred Haney of not wanting to sign black players. "What hurts us more than anything else is that Fred Haney apparently doesn't want Negros at Hollywood, and he is leading the pack without them."[16] There is no direct evidence showing whether Fred Haney decided not to sign black players because of their race; as the manager of a winning team, he was likely not looking for new players to add to the roster. Haney managed the Hollywood Stars from 1949 to 1952. During that period the team signed only two black players, one for only a few months.

Managers began to move between Major and Minor League assignments, sometimes coming to the PCL already having worked with players of color. In 1951 Joe Gordon managed the Sacramento Solons. Three seasons earlier he was a teammate of Satchel Paige on the World Series–winning Cleveland Indians. Gordon voted in favor of the Cleveland Indians giving Paige a full share of the World Series money.[17] Gordon joined the Sacramento Solons the year after they integrated, so it would appear that he either supported integration or did not object to it. Also in 1951, the *Los Angeles Sentinel* speculated about the amount of influence held by a manager in adding a black player to the team roster when making a prediction about Los Angeles Angels manager Stan Hack on his possible promotion to manager of the Chicago Cubs. "Although Hack has done a good job with the Angels this season, the 'peculiarity' of this style insofar as Negro players are concerned forces one to wonder if [Hack's] promotion won't kill whatever chance Gene Baker will have with the Cubs." By 1956 the worries were unfounded, as the *Los Angeles Sentinel* reported: "[Chicago Cubs] Manager Stan Hack is said to be counting on his Negro stars to keep the Cubs well up in the National League race."[18] Gene Baker was a member of that 1956 Chicago Cubs team.

The black press suspected southern-born managers, in particular, of racism. In 1951 and 1952 Mel Ott managed the Oakland Oaks. The allowance of black players on the team appeared to the *Los Angeles Sentinel* to be a shift in policy for the Louisiana-born Ott. In 1947 "[Ott] was quoted as having said that no Negro players would be signed by the Giants as long as he had anything to do with it."[19] Instead, Ott would manage an integrated team.

Managing a team with African American players may or may not have changed a white manager's opinions about race. In 1956 in an article in the *Los Angeles Sentinel*, L. I. "Brock" Brockenbury rejoiced at the dismissal of the Mississippi-born Clay Hopper. Manager of the Portland Beavers from 1952 to 1955 and the Hollywood Stars in 1956, Hopper was Branch Rickey's handpicked choice to manage the Montreal Royals in 1946, the year the team integrated with Jackie Robinson. Rickey likely would not have selected Hopper if he did not believe that Hopper would support integration.[20] However, in 1956 in an article for the *Chicago Defender*, Brockenbury wrote, "Another one I'm glad to see leave these parts is Clay Hopper, the guy who despite being Jackie Robinsons [*sic*] first manager in organized baseball never could get used to Negroes being in baseball. . . . Don't believe me, huh? Ask some of the guys who played for him, including Robinson and Sam Jethroe, what they thought about him. . . . Why do you think Lino Donoso [*sic*] quit last year?"[21]

Whether the *Chicago Defender* accurately summarized Clay Hopper's interactions with black players is difficult to assess from one article, but it is the most negative description of a white manger's racial views published in the *Los Angeles Sentinel* or the *Chicago Defender* from 1948 to 1957. Managers could greatly influence the experience that players of color had on a team. Experienced players would have to prove themselves to more than just managers to find acceptance.

For some of the players who integrated a team in the PCL, breaking down the color line in baseball would take more than one try. Born February 12, 1923, in Houston, Marvin Williams had a tryout with the Red Sox in 1945, played baseball for nineteen years on teams in the Negro and Mexican Leagues, and had a career in the Minors. "Tex" Williams was an infielder and outfielder. He played semipro baseball in and around Conroe, Texas. When he was twenty-three Williams participated in two games with the local team against the barnstorming Negro League team the Philadelphia Stars. Williams played so well that the Stars wanted him to join the team. Williams recalled that he left to join the Philadelphia Stars on June 23, 1943, and continued playing baseball until 1962.[22] In 1944 he changed his position from shortstop to second base to accommodate Frank Austin, who went on to integrate the Portland Beavers.[23] The move did not hurt Williams, as he played in the East-West All-Star Game in 1944.

Of the April 1945 Boston Red Sox tryout organized by Wendell Smith, Williams recalled that the three had trouble checking into their hotel in Boston. The hotel would not honor their reservation, and a white man offered his home. The tryout included infield practice and batting practice with nonstarting Red Sox players.[24] Each man played for Negro League teams, and each would integrate a team in organized ball: for Sam Jethroe and Jackie Robinson it would be Major League teams; for Williams it would be a Minor League team. Each of the three players attempted more than once to gain access to what organized baseball denied them before integration. For Marvin Williams that chance came five years later. On August 23, 1950, the Sacramento Solons signed the twenty-seven-year-old second basemen. On August 24 the *Sacramento Bee* quoted Solon general manager Jo Jo White: "In an effort to build a winning club for Sacramento, I have sought capable baseball material from whatever source they could be obtained without reference to religion or race.... I am especially happy that we have just now obtained Marvin Williams, Negro second baseman, and who, although I have not seen him play, comes most highly recommended. He will be given every opportunity to demonstrate his ability to make good in the Pacific Coast League."[25] In addition, the article included Williams's baseball career, giving the previous teams he played for and in what years. This newspaper article included more information than any other newspaper article describing a player who integrated one of the PCL teams. In most cases the player was just identified as being black with no other information about the player.

Once teams began adding players of color to their rosters, they frequently signed several. The day after signing Marvin Williams, the Solons inked a contract with African American pitcher Walter McCoy. After pitching for the Chicago American Giants from 1945 to 1948, McCoy, a twenty-six-year-old San Diego native, pitched eight games for the Visalia Cubs of the California League, a Chicago Cubs affiliate, in 1949. Marvin Williams and Walter McCoy traveled from winter ball in Venezuela to join the Solons. Williams played in the first game of the doubleheader on Sunday, August 27, 1950. McCoy first pitched two days later in Sacramento. As two or three players joined the first player, players of color could have a real impact on the attitudes of the team management and other players.

With more than 60 percent of PCL teams integrated in 1950 and teams in six other new Minor Leagues signing players of color, momentum seemed to be on the side of change. In Washington DC, Secretary of the Interior Oscar L. Chapman integrated that city's swimming pools. The Supreme Court issued three decisions on June 5, 1950, that overturned segregation. *McLaurin v. Oklahoma* overturned segregation in graduate or professional education. In *Sweatt v. Painter*, the decision challenged the doctrine of separate but equal by stating that a separate law school for African Americans established in Texas was not equal to the school for white students. Also on that date the court abolished segregation in railroad dining cars in the *Henderson v. United States* decision. Legal challenges to the system of segregation continued to break down barriers in society.

In the traditional definition of integration, a player playing for a team only during spring training does not "count" as the player who integrated a team. Only regular-season games count for statistics and integration. Frank Barnes spent more time with the San Francisco Seals during spring training than the one game he pitched in during the regular season. Other players of color participated in spring training, and, in fact, for most of spring training it appears that Bob Thurman would be the one to integrate the team.

Born in Longwood, Mississippi, on August 26, 1928, Frank Barnes's sixteen years in professional baseball included pitching in fifteen games at the Major League level with the St. Louis Cardinals. Barnes's baseball career began in 1949 with the Kansas City Monarchs. The right-hander pitched in the Negro Leagues for two seasons. On July 24, 1950, the New York Yankees signed Barnes and sent him to their Single-A affiliate the Muskegon Clippers of the Central League. The Yankees also signed Elston Howard from the Monarchs.[26] Barnes and Elston were the fourth and fifth black players the Yankees signed to contracts,[27] after Luis Márquez, Frank Austin, and Artie Wilson, but none of the players had yet made it to the Yankee roster.[28] Before the 1951 season Barnes's contract was sold to the Binghamton Triplets, another Single-A affiliate of the Yankees, and to the San Francisco Seals on February 11, 1951.

Frank Barnes was not the only black player the Seals wanted to try out at spring training in Modesto in March 1951. Manager Lefty O'Doul waited for Barnes as well as Elston Howard, Barney Serrell, and Bob Thurman.[29] On March 4 the *San Francisco Chronicle* reported that Serrell and Alonzo Perry, of the Birmingham Black Barons, were in camp on a thirty-day conditional basis and that Thurman had arrived on a late-afternoon plane.[30] Thurman checked into camp the next day. He was the first African American with whom the Seals signed a contract.[31]

Born in Wichita, Kansas, on May 14, 1917, Robert Burns Thurman experienced a baseball career that included the Negro Leagues, the Minor Leagues, winter ball in Puerto Rico, and five seasons in the Majors. After five years of military service in the Pacific theater of World War II, the outfielder returned home to play for the Homestead Grays from 1946 to 1948. In 1949 he was with the Kansas City Monarchs when the Yankees signed him midseason, making him one of the team's first black players. The Yankees sent him to the Newark Bears of the International League. The next year he played 145 games for the Springfield Cubs. When Thurman arrived at spring training for the San Francisco Seals in 1951, the coverage noted his physique. "Perfectly proportioned, isn't he," said manager Lefty O'Doul of his six-foot-two, 199-pound outfielder. "He looks as though he has done all the things they say he has, and can do all the things they say he will."[32] What O'Doul did not know was that Thurman had taken four years off his age. Thurman, like other Negro League players whom organized baseball segregated during the peak of their careers, was trying to break into a league while competing with younger players.

As Thurman impressed the Seals, Frank Barnes and Elston Howard, among others, had not yet arrived in camp. Bob Thurman's signed contract arrived in the Seals' mail on March 6, 1951.[33] The Yankees optioned Barnes's contract to the Seals for a thirty-day look. As spring-training games continued, it seemed as though Thurman would be the one to integrate the Seals when the season opened. The *San Francisco Chronicle* profiled him, his bat helped win spring-training games, and, more than once, the press labeled him as the first black player to sign a contract with the Seals.

Frank Barnes arrived in Modesto and participated in his first spring-training workout on March 13. At first thinking Barnes to be a no-show, Bob Stevens ranked the pitcher second to Bob Thurman as the best new player.[34] However, when the Seals prepared to open the 1951 season in San Diego, Thurman stayed home with an injured hand and did not go down in history as the one who integrated the Seals. On March 31, 1951, Frank Barnes pitched in relief in Los Angeles as the Angels ended San Francisco's winning streak at five games. The *San Francisco Chronicle* did not make any reference of his race or historic accomplishment, although the *Los Angeles Times* did with the note that "Frank Barnes became the first Negro ever to play a PCL game for the Seals yesterday when he followed Savage and Savarese on the hill."[35] The next day Barney Serrell, a second baseman for the Kansas City Monarchs for six seasons and a player in the Mexican Leagues, had one at bat. Serrell played in sixty-two games for San Francisco in 1951. It was not until April 3 that Bob Thurman played in a regular-season game. The man who appeared throughout spring training to be the one who would integrate the Seals was the third African American player they fielded.

On the same day Thurman debuted, the Seals sold the contract of Alonzo Perry, a former Negro Leaguer who played for the Oakland Oaks in 1949, to the Kansas City Blues.[36] Frank Barnes made his final appearance as a Seal on Friday, April 13. After San Francisco Barnes returned to Muskegon through Binghamton in the middle of April. In July he traveled from Muskegon to Kansas City and in July moved up to the Toronto Maple Leafs. Although Frank Barnes was a San Francisco Seal for only two games, he received recognition as the one who integrated the team. During that limited time he could not have interacted with other players off the baseball diamond and influenced their opinions about race.

It seemed that Frank Barnes, Barney Serrell, or Bob Thurman could not change the opinions of their manager Lefty O'Doul. Born in San Francisco in 1897, Francis Joseph "Lefty" O'Doul played Major League Baseball in New York, Boston, and Philadelphia. He managed the San Francisco Seals for seventeen years, from 1937 to 1951. San Francisco was the sixth team to integrate, and that may have been, in part, because of O'Doul. In 1948 the San Francisco Seals promised two black players, Curtis Roberts and Gene Richardson, a tryout with the team. On March 7, 1948, the *Chicago Defender* reported that while general manager Charles Graham Jr. was willing to proceed with a tryout, club president Charles Graham Sr. and manager Lefty O'Doul were not.[37] A year later, on March 5, 1949, the *Chicago Defender* reports that the "Oakland Seals [*sic*] . . . signed a Negro pitcher, Percy Fisher." The short article then goes on to say, "The team manager announced to his players that those who do not approve playing with a Negro can quit now. He said he will hire more Negros when he finds capable players."[38] Percy Fisher never appeared in the San Francisco Seals' lineup. In 1949 he joined the Redding (CA) Browns of the Far West League, a Class D league. He pitched in twenty-six games for the Redding Browns, a team not affiliated with the Seals. For the 1950 season Fisher pitched in twenty-five games for the Salt Lake City Bees of the Class C Pioneer League, also a team not affiliated with the Seals.

It is difficult to know if Lefty O'Doul was sincere when he said that the other players had to accept Percy Fisher when Fisher did not then join the team. Barney Serrell was certain, however, of his memories of O'Doul. Barry Mednick, who interviewed Serrell between November 1994 and July 1996, recorded Serrell's experience with O'Doul: "What should have been the highlight of my career became a disaster. The source of my problems was the Seals' manager Lefty O'Doul. . . . Lefty was a racist and didn't try to hide his feelings." While the *San Francisco Chronicle* reported that O'Doul admired Thurman's physique, Serrell remembered it differently: "I arrived with Bob Thurman and we were introduced to O'Doul. . . . A Seals executive escorted us onto the field. No sooner did O'Doul see us then he said, 'I told you to get ballplayers, not monkeys!' The remark hurt me, but I said nothing at the time. Things just got worse from there. O'Doul would let black players cash our checks in his bar, then he would not even let us get a beer. Cash the check, then we would have to go."[39]

As Serrell told it, O'Doul was not subtle in his racism. The San Francisco-born manager held beliefs that were not the sole property of the South. O'Doul was another example of how racism was not absent from the West Coast. His attitude reinforced the fact that minorities could never be sure what they would have to deal with from person to person. O'Doul even required Serrell and Thurman to perform in a way that worked against the team winning. "O'Doul would tell me to foul off four pitches before trying to put the ball into play. Why would anyone deliberately foul off pitches when he can get a hit? But if I failed to get four foul balls, I was taken from the game. One day, Bob Thurman hit a home run on a hit and run play. O'Doul yanked him from the game. O'Doul angrily informed Thurman that you don't hit home runs on a hit and run. Now, why would anyone complain about a two run homer?"[40]

After this treatment from O'Doul, Serrell was sent by the Seals to their farm club in Yakima, Washington. The Yakima Bears, a Class B team in the Western International League, sent Serrell back to the Seals, saying he was too good.[41] The actions of O'Doul show that some managers made decisions about players based on race, even if it was detrimental to the team.

Lefty O'Doul was on the forefront of the relationship between professional baseball in the United States and Japan. In October 1931 an All-Star team that included O'Doul, as a player, played seventeen games against Japanese teams in Japan. The next year O'Doul returned to Japan with Moe Berg, a catcher with the Washington Senators, and Ted Lyons, a pitcher with the Chicago White Sox.[42] The three Americans coached Japanese players at Tokyo universities, and O'Doul encouraged the Japanese to form a professional league. In 1934 O'Doul returned as part of a team that included Babe Ruth. After World War II Lefty O'Doul, now manager of the San Francisco Seals, returned to Japan in 1949 for a six-week tour with his PCL team that played an important role in improving postwar relations between the United States and Japan. Of the tour General Matthew Ridgway, the military governor of Japan, said, "Words cannot describe Lefty's wonderful contributions through baseball to the post-war rebuilding effort."[43] Lefty O'Doul returned with Major Leaguers in 1951. In 1953 he brought a Japanese team to play in the United States. For his relationship with Japanese baseball, the San Francisco sportswriters named O'Doul the "Father of Baseball in Japan."[44]

In 1950 Herman Wedemeyer and Wally Yonamine, two Asian American football players, attempted to join PCL rosters. Both tried to join the San Francisco Seals; neither had a successful tryout. Wedemeyer, of Native Hawaiian and Chinese ancestry, and Yonamine, of Native Hawaiian and Japanese ancestry, both arrived in the Seal training camp on February 20, 1950.[45] Wedemeyer did not make the Seals but played in the Minor Leagues with the Yakima Bears and Salt Lake City Bees in the spring of 1950.[46] Articles in the *Los Angeles Times* included two references to his size, "squat" and "little."[47] Before he became the first American to play professional baseball in Japan after World War II, Yonamine attempted to join the San Francisco Seals.[48] He too went to the Salt Lake City Bees, playing 123 games with them in 1950. In the post–World War II West, as Japanese Americans were rebuilding their lives after life in internment camps, PCL teams did not exclude Asian Americans in the same way as blacks before integration, but after 1948 owners and managers did not include them on rosters.

Many of the players who integrated the Pacific Coast League had previous professional baseball experience, but that did not automatically qualify them to play in the Major Leagues. Many of the players entering into the Minor Leagues had already passed the peak of their careers or were now older than average Major League players. Born December 6, 1913, in Atlanta, Roy Horace Welmaker was an all-star baseball player in high school. Welmaker graduated from Clark College in Atlanta with a bachelor of science degree. Welmaker's professional baseball career began in 1930 with the Atlanta Black Crackers and then the Macon Black Peaches. The southpaw's Negro League tenure fully began with the Homestead Grays after his graduation from Clark College in 1937. Welmaker also pitched in the Mexican League, the Venezuelan League, and while in the army. At Fort Benning, Georgia, Welmaker made headlines when he struck out forty-nine batters in twenty-three innings in less than twenty-four hours.[49] He pitched in seven Negro League World Series.

On April 11, 1949, the Cleveland Indians signed Welmaker to a contract. In preseason play in exhibition games in Los Angeles, Welmaker tried to gain a spot on the regular-season roster, pitching for the Indians in the last week of the season.[50] Cleveland sent Welmaker to the Wilkes-Barre Indians, their Single-A affiliate in the Eastern League, where he played in thirty-six games. Winning twenty-two games earned Welmaker a plane ticket from Atlanta to Ontario to fight for a spot on Cleveland's Triple-A affiliate, the San Diego Padres, for the 1950 season.[51] He did well in spring training and made the team. Of the fourteen black players in the PCL that year, the San Diego roster had four, all of whom opened the season.

Welmaker was the starting pitcher in the third game of the 1950 season on March 30 in San Diego. He gave up four hits to the visiting San Francisco Seals and came out of the game in the ninth inning. After Welmaker's fourth straight victory, Al Wolf of the *Los Angeles Times* stated, "The colored southpaw became the loop's [PCL's] undisputed pitching leader." This was the first notation of Welmaker's race that the *Times* included. Welmaker pitched in forty-seven games for San Diego in 1950. He also had to admit that his actual age was not twenty-nine but thirty-six.[52] Like other players from the Negro Leagues, Welmaker knew his true age might prevent him from having a chance to play in organized ball. His skill on the mound helped bring forgiveness.

Before spring training in January 1951, reporter Bob Lantz noted that Roy Welmaker was the first Padre to sign his contract for the upcoming season. He also speculated that the pitcher had received a raise after his 1950 season ended with a record of 16-10.[53] On May 7, 1951, after one win and one loss with San Diego, the Hollywood Stars purchased Welmaker's contract. Welmaker joined the team on May 9 and pitched, for the first time as a Star, in relief on May 11. It marked the integration of the Hollywood Stars and left the Seattle Rainiers as the only team lacking any players of color. On May 16 Welmaker pitched one and two-thirds innings in relief, and on May 21 he started his first game for Hollywood. Welmaker finished the season in Hollywood. In 1952 the Stars released Welmaker on April 27, and the Portland Beavers signed him on May 6. Roy Welmaker, Ed Steele in 1952, and John Ritchey in 1955 were the only three African American or Latino players signed by the Hollywood Stars between 1948 and 1957. With just two players playing in three different seasons, Hollywood was just above the minimum levels of integration.

The Seattle Rainiers became the eighth and final team of the PCL to integrate on April 1, 1952. The press, however, had mistakenly reported that the team integrated the year before with John Ford Smith. On March 22, 1951, the *Los Angeles Sentinel* reported that the Hollywood Stars were the eighth and final PCL team without black players on the roster.[54] Smith, an Arizona native, had played eight seasons in the Negro Leagues. The Seattle Rainiers invited him to spring training for a tryout. The *Los Angeles Times* noted that Smith was "the first [black] player ever to work out with the Seattle club."[55] On March 6 Smith joined the team.[56] In his pitching debut with the Rainiers, Smith gave up seven hits and four runs.[57] The day before the final exhibition game of spring training, Smith and the Seattle Rainiers could not come to an agreement about the contract, and Smith left camp.[58] Seattle Rainiers manager Rogers Hornsby said, "Smith wanted a bonus for signing with us. We were willing to give him the bonus, but he wasn't willing to wait the 30 days for us to look at him."[59] Another theory was that Smith did not like that the contract did not have a clause about injuries.[60] Since John Ford Smith played for the Seattle Rainiers only during spring-training games and not during the regular season, he did not integrate the team.

Given the background of Rogers Hornsby, though, the failed contractual agreement may be more than just a disagreement about money. *The Sporting News* reported that the Texas-born Hornsby had been a member of the Ku Klux Klan.[61] In 1945 the *Chicago Defender* reported that when he was manager of the Vera Cruz Blues of the Mexican Leagues, Hornsby quit because the owner would not fire African American player Willie Wells Sr. and three other black players. The article quoted Hornsby as saying that "Negro players ought to stay in their own league where they belong. . . . 'They've [African Americans] been getting along all right playing together.'" In August 1946 the *Defender* noted that "Rogers Hornsby . . . returned from Mexico when he couldn't inject the anti-Negro spirit into the Mexican owners." On March 22, 1951, when the Seattle Rainiers looked ready to sign Smith, the *Los Angeles Sentinel* reported, "The signing of Ford Smith represents quite a 'change of heart' for Rogers Hornsby, according to popular reports from a few years ago."[62] Maybe the discussion of the price of the contract was a simple disagreement, but there is also the possibility that Hornsby attempted to sign a black player but knew it would never actually happen.

Hornsby was not the first Seattle manager to express a desire to keep the team white only. From 1946 to 1949 Georgia native Jo Jo White managed the Rainiers. He expressed to the team that he would not "mix with blacks."[63]

In 1951 Rainiers owner Emil Sick hired Rogers Hornsby to manage the Seattle team. As the new manager of the last team in the PCL without a player of color, Hornsby told *The Sporting News*, "We would be very happy to have a Negro player on our team if we could find one who would help us."[64] This was the same excuse used by the Major League teams like the Boston Red Sox to explain why they had not signed a player of color when many others already had.

The Rainiers would finally sign and play two players of color to start the 1952 season, becoming the eighth and final PCL team to integrate. Their new manager, Bill Sweeney, integrated with two players rather than one. Bob Boyd and Artie Wilson each joined the Seattle Rainiers, having come from other PCL teams. By 1952 each PCL team had formalized a relationship with a Major League team. According to team records, in December 1947 the Seattle Rainiers entered into an affiliate agreement with the Detroit Tigers.[65] The agreement included the expectation that the Tigers would send the Rainiers players by March 15, 1948. The Detroit Tigers would become the second-to-last Major League team to integrate, playing Ozzie Virgil on June 6, 1958.[66] The management of the Rainiers may have expected players as part of their agreement, but the Detroit Tigers did not send players of color down to their affiliate.

By the November 26, 1951, Board of Directors meeting, the Seattle Rainiers had contracted with the Chicago White Sox, a team that had integrated in 1951 with former PCL San Diego Padre Minnie Miñoso. In the minutes of the board meeting, team general manager and vice president Earl Sheely reported on the prospect for the Rainiers to receive players from the White Sox for the next season. He stated that "the Club's relations with the Chicago White Sox of the American League were very satisfactory and that he expected to get help from them for next season. He also discussed the possibility of acquiring one or two negro players for next season." Since the statement that the White Sox might send two African American players is included in the same sentence as the fact that the relationship with the White Sox was very satisfactory, one has to assume the Rainiers had no problem with receiving black players and even wanted them on the team roster. In the next paragraph team vice president R. C. Torrance reported on the issues of televising games. There was no discussion noted, positive or negative, about the possible receipt of black players. In the minutes of the Rainiers' stockholders meeting on April 9, 1952, Sheely stated that the present personnel of the Rainiers were "in sound position except for its pitching, and that he hoped to receive player help from the White Sox in the near future."[67] This statement clearly shows that Minor League teams expected their Major League affiliate to send them players.

The first player that the Chicago White Sox sent to the Rainiers was Bob Boyd. Robert Boyd signed his first contract with organized baseball on August 4, 1950. Born in Potts Camp, Mississippi, in 1925, Boyd was a four-year veteran of the Negro Leagues, playing first base for the Memphis Red Sox. He was the first black player to sign a contract with the Chicago White Sox, but he did not become the first player of color to play for the team. During the 1950 and 1951 seasons, Boyd worked his way through the White Sox's Minor League system. Going first to the Colorado Springs Sky Sox of the Western League, Chicago's Single-A affiliate, Boyd was then optioned by the White Sox to the Sacramento Solons. He joined the Solons, the White Sox's Triple-A affiliate, on Saturday, March 24, 1951. On September 2 the Chicago White Sox recalled Boyd. Bob Boyd made his White Sox debut on September 8, 1951, playing in twelve games in the final month of the season. Joining former PCL player Minnie Miñoso on the White Sox roster, Boyd would play nine seasons in the Majors. Before the season opened the next year, on March 21, 1952, the White Sox optioned Boyd to their new Minor League affiliate, the Seattle Rainiers.

Boyd was not the only black player to join the Seattle Rainiers in March 1952. In the fall of 1950, the New York Giants purchased Artie Wilson's contract, and he played nineteen games in the first part of the 1951 season. The team sent Wilson to Triple-A Ottawa in May. In late June the New York Giants optioned Wilson's contract to the Oakland Oaks, and the former batting champion made a return trip to the East Bay.

The Chicago White Sox, having purchased Artie Wilson's contract in December 1951, sent him to spring training the following year. The team looked forward to Wilson's arrival at training camp in Palm Springs, California. Seattle expected Boyd in Palm Springs, but it was Wilson who arrived first, on March 12, 1952. Boyd arrived during the last week of spring training, on March 24, 1952. Both Boyd and Wilson played in the Seattle opener in Hollywood, thus integrating the final team of the PCL. Each player had five at bats and three hits. With Boyd and Wilson, all of the teams of the PCL had now signed and played a player of color, thereby integrating the entire league.

Four years and one day after Bill Starr sent John Ritchey onto the baseball diamond as a San Diego Padre, the eighth and final Pacific Coast League integrated. The teams of the PCL were not the first to integrate, but they became the first league to integrate each team. The process of integration forced individual players to achieve their professional dreams while also managing racism and discrimination. The players of color each sacrificed their safety and experienced isolation while breaking down racial barriers in each city in which they played. The consequences of the actions of those who participated in integration were seen on not only the baseball diamond but throughout the larger society as well. As each of the teams of the Pacific Coast League signed players of color, they joined a mass movement for social change, the long and wide civil rights movement. In the 1940s and 1950s the signing of players of color was no longer an event that lasted a day or two or required players to misrepresent their race to join the team. As players of color joined the rosters on Major and Minor League teams, they participated in a larger shift in society. The change happened when individual players had the opportunity to prove their athleticism on an equal basis. Sometimes that process happened easily, and sometimes it required great personal sacrifice. Their experience in baseball at all levels, from the Negro Leagues to the Mexican Leagues to winter ball, helped make them professionals who could individually and collectively face the challenges of racism and discrimination. They were each part of a movement that had developed such momentum from 1948 to 1952 that it could only continue forward.

AFTERWORD

The integration of the Pacific Coast League was part of a larger movement for social change in the United States. The individuals who took part changed not only their sport but American society as well. The players who integrated eight teams of the Pacific Coast League continued to play baseball, married and raised families, and had second careers. Society would only sometimes remember the many players who broke the color line as a professional baseball player and almost never as a player who integrated a team of the Pacific Coast League. This afterword includes a brief look at their careers and lives after integration. None of the players became a public activist for racial change after their baseball careers as Jackie Robinson did. Most found work in jobs not related to sports and raised families without the recognition of their part in historical events.

JOHN RITCHEY

Over his career Ritchey played two years (1948, 1949) for the Padres, two years (1950, 1951) for the Portland Beavers, two years (1951, 1952) in Vancouver of the Western International League, two years (1953, 1954) for the Sacramento Solons, a year (1955) for the San Francisco Seals, and his last year (1956) in Syracuse for the International League. Over his seven seasons in the PCL, Ritchey hit .282. He played catcher with some time in the outfield, and he played winter ball in Venezuela. His experiences in Canada and South America were better than those in the United States. "In 1951, I was player of the year for Vancouver. We were happy there. The fans were good and there was acceptance. And it was very comfortable to play in South America. I always played my best when I was happy and all I ever wanted to do was play baseball."[1] When he retired from professional baseball after playing on seven teams between 1948 and 1956, John Ritchey worked as a milkman and deliveryman while playing sandlot baseball and handball. He suffered a stroke and died in January 2003. Ritchey had been married to his wife, Lydia, for fifty-five years. They had three children. Ritchey's family traveled with him throughout his career. Today Ritchey's smile is seen in his granddaughter's face.

ARTIE WILSON

Wilson played as a Seattle Rainier for the 1952–54 seasons, spent 1955 and 1956 in Portland, and went to Sacramento for the 1957 and 1958 seasons. He returned to the Portland Beavers in 1962. After his baseball career ended, Wilson lived in Portland, working in sales at Gary Worth Lincoln-Mercury car dealership in Gladstone, Oregon. He married Dorothy Daniels in 1949, and they had three children, Jean, Zoe, and Artie II. Artie Wilson died on October 31, 2010, after a struggle with Alzheimer's disease. Until the end of his life, Wilson rooted for the San Francisco Giants.[2]

FRANK AUSTIN

From May 23, 1949, to April 5, 1956, Frank Austin was under contract with the Portland Beavers. During his career as a Beavers shortstop, he batted .267 with 29 home runs and 258 runs batted in. In 1955, at the last game Portland played in the beloved stadium on Vaughn Street, the team's Most Popular Player was Frank Austin.[3] Austin then played the 1956 season for the PCL's Vancouver Mounties and ended his career the following year when the Louisville Colonels of the American Association released him on April 9, 1957. Austin died three years later, on January 15, 1960, in Panama City, Panama.

LUIS MÁRQUEZ

Luis Márquez played 68 games for the Major League Boston Braves, batting .197. Sent to the Minors, Márquez played in Milwaukee and Toledo before the

Chicago Cubs drafted him in 1953. Márquez began the 1954 season with the Cubs, but they traded him to the Pittsburgh Pirates. In 31 games he batted only .095. Márquez returned to Portland in 1955, playing there until 1958. After 109 games he went to Dallas and, after his playing days ended, became a scout for Montreal in the Caribbean. In 1988 Luis Ramos, his son-in-law, shot him twice after an argument. He died on February 1, 1988.[4]

BOOKER MCDANIELS

After integrating the Los Angeles Angels in June 1949, Booker McDaniels would play fifty-five games for the team. The Angels sold McDaniels's contract to their Single-A affiliate, the Des Moines Bruins of the Western League.[5] McDaniels played for the Mexico City Red Devils in 1951, his last year in professional baseball. Booker McDaniels died on December 12, 1974, in Kansas City, Missouri, of throat cancer.

MARVIN WILLIAMS

After integrating Sacramento Marvin Williams played in the Negro National League, the Arizona-Texas League, the Gulf Coast League, the Mexican Leagues, the Western International League, the South Atlantic (or Sally) League, and the Texas League. In 1955 he returned to Seattle for part of the season. During his eleven seasons in the Minors, Williams had a batting average of .316. Marvin Williams died on December 23, 2000, in Conroe, Texas.

FRANK BARNES

After pitching for two innings for the San Francisco Seals, Frank Barnes played for numerous teams: Binghamton, New York; Muskegon, Michigan; Kansas City, Kansas; Toronto; Scranton, Pennsylvania; Charleston; Oklahoma City; Minneapolis; Omaha; St. Louis; Rochester, New York; Chicago; San Diego; Portland; Indianapolis; Buffalo; Little Rock, Arkansas; Reynosa, Mexico; and Seattle. Barnes's professional baseball career ended on January 1970. During those twenty-four years Barnes pitched in fifteen games over three seasons for the Major League St. Louis Cardinals, in 1957, 1958, and 1960. Frank Barnes married Juanita Harris in 1950, and they had two sons. He owned and operated a pool hall in the off-seasons. Frank Barnes died on October 19, 2014, in Grenville, Mississippi.

ROY WELMAKER

In 1953 Welmaker returned to Hollywood and ended his PCL and baseball career there after eight games. Welmaker married three times and did not have any children. He owned and operated Welmaker's Service Station and auto parts store in Los Angeles until retiring in the 1980s. Welmaker moved to Decatur, Georgia, in 1994, the same year he was inducted into the Clark Atlanta University Hall of Fame.[6] Roy Welmaker died on February 3, 1998, in Decatur, Georgia.

BOB BOYD

During the 1952 season the Seattle Rainiers placed Bob Boyd on the disabled list from April 24 to May 7, 1952. By August they optioned his contract to the Chicago White Sox. He would play nine seasons for Major League teams, including the Baltimore Orioles, the Kansas City Athletics, and the Milwaukee Braves. His last Major League game was September 24, 1961. He played in the Minor Leagues for another three seasons. Bob Boyd married twice, first to Elizabeth Miller in 1946 and then to Valca Terrell in 1952. Bob and Valca Boyd celebrated their fiftieth wedding anniversary at the Negro Leagues Baseball Museum in Kansas City, Missouri. After retiring from his twenty-year career as an MTA bus driver in Wichita, Kansas, Boyd was diagnosed with diabetes and lost his right leg to the disease. Bob Boyd died on September 7, 2004. His obituary listed "Bobby" Boyd as a retired MTA bus driver and former professional baseball player.[7]

THE END OF THE "OLD COAST LEAGUE"

The Pacific Coast League in its original organization would last only five seasons beyond the 1952 season. In 1957 the owners of the Brooklyn Dodgers and the New York Giants agreed to move their teams to Los Angeles and San Francisco, respectively. For Brooklyn and New York it meant the loss of two professional baseball teams, but for the West Coast it was the beginning of hometown Major League teams. Air travel meant that teams could make the journey across the continent and spread Major League Baseball to new regions of the country. While many fans welcomed the arrival of the two teams, others knew it meant the end of the Pacific Coast League. The "Old

Coast League," as the league from 1903 to 1957 is now known, could not compete with the Majors. In 1952 it appeared that the PCL might become a third Major League when Major League Baseball changed its classification from Triple-A to "open," a new category created for the PCL. With declining attendance, smaller ballparks than the Majors, and then the arrival of the Major Leagues on the West Coast, the PCL was not to join MLB but faced the end of an era.

The eight teams of the original Pacific Coast League either disbanded or relocated, beginning with the Oakland Oaks, who moved to Vancouver in 1956. The Pacific Coast League did continue after 1957 and played the 1958 season with its Triple-A classification reinstated. In 1958 the reconfigured PCL teams included the Phoenix Giants, Portland Beavers, Sacramento Solons, Salt Lake City Bees, San Diego Padres, Seattle Rainiers, Spokane Indians, and Vancouver Mounties. No longer located only in the Pacific Coast states of California, Oregon, and Washington, the PCL today includes a total of sixteen teams in thirteen states as far east as Iowa, Louisiana, and Tennessee.

On March 30, 2005, the San Diego Padres, a Major League team since 1969, held a ceremony in which a bronze bust of John Ritchey was unveiled at Petco Park. The John Ritchey Task Force collected enough money to cast the bronze bust of Ritchey to honor the player and the history of the Old Coast League. It serves as a fitting memorial to the man who faced the challenges of a segregated league and became a pioneer for racial equality by playing a game.

APPENDIX

TABLE 1. PACIFIC COAST LEAGUE INTEGRATION BY TEAM

PCL team	Players	Date of integration
San Diego Padres	John Ritchey	March 30, 1948
Oakland Oaks	Artie Wilson	May 22, 1949
Portland Beavers	Frank Austin Luis Márquez	May 24, 1949
Los Angeles Angels	Booker McDaniels	June 15, 1949
Sacramento Solons	Marvin Williams	August 27, 1950
San Francisco Seals	Frank Barnes	March 31, 1951
Hollywood Stars	Roy Welmaker	May 11, 1951
Seattle Rainiers	Bob Boyd Artie Wilson	April 1, 1952

Sources: Date of integration from my own research.

TABLE 2. PACIFIC COAST LEAGUE PLAYERS OF ASIAN ANCESTRY TO 1959

Name	PCL years	Ethnicity
Barney Joy	1907	½ Native Hawaiian/ Chinese
John B. "Honolulu Johnnie" Williams	1911–15	¼ Native Hawaiian
Lang Akana	1915	Chinese American (born in Hawaii)
Henry Oana	1929–34	½ Native Hawaiian, ½ Portuguese
Lee Gum Hong (Albert Bowen)	1932	Chinese American
Kenso Nushida	1932	Japanese American
Clarence Kumalae	1933 (tryout)	Native Hawaiian
Fumito "Jimmy" Horio	1935	Japanese American (born in Hawaii)
John M. "Johnny" Kerr	1936	Native Hawaiian/ Chinese
Herman Wedemeyer	1950 (tryout)	Native Hawaiian/ Chinese
Wally Yonamine	1950 (tryout)	Native Hawaiian/ Japanese
Robert Rudolph Balcena	1955–58	Filipino American

Sources: PCL years from baseball-reference.com and my own research. Ethnicity from Joel S. Franks, *Crossing Sidelines, Crossing Cultures: Sport and Asian Pacific American Cultural Citizenship* (Lanham MD: University Press of America, 2000); and my own research.

TABLE 3. PACIFIC COAST LEAGUE PLAYERS OF
NATIVE AMERICAN ANCESTRY TO 1959

Name	PCL years	Tribe
Elijah "Ed" Pinnance	1908–9	Ojibwe
John "Indian" House	1909	Oneida
George Howard "Chief" Johnson	1916–18	Ho-Chunk/Winnebago
Luther C. "Indian" Smith	1916–20	Unknown
James Francis "Jim" Thorpe	1922	Sac and Fox
Moses J. "Mose" YellowHorse	1923–24	Pawnee
Frank D. Tincup	1943–45	Cherokee

Sources: Players and tribal information from Jeffrey Powers-Beck, *The American Indian Integration of Baseball* (Lincoln: University of Nebraska Press, 2004); and Joel S. Franks, *The National Pastime and Cultural Diversity in California, 1858-1941* (Lanham MD: Scarecrow Press, 2001).

TABLE 4. PACIFIC COAST LEAGUE PLAYERS
OF LATIN ANCESTRY TO 1959

Name	PCL years	Country of birth
Jesse Sandoval Flores	1939–42, 1948–54	Mexico
Froilan "Nanny" Fernandez	1940–41, 1952–55	United States
Manuel Ruiz "Manny" Perez	1942, 1946, 1948–51	United States
Manuel P. "Nay" Hernandez	1944	United States
Saturnino Orestes Armas "Minnie" Miñoso Arrieta	1949, 1950	Cuba
Luis Márquez	1949–50, 1955–58	Puerto Rico
Frank Austin	1949–56	Panama
José Bache	1950	Mexico
Manuel Echeveria	1950	Mexico
Rafael Miguel "Ray" Noble	1950, 1952	Cuba
Lorenzo Cabrera	1951	Cuba
Alejandro Eloy "Álex" Carrasquel Aparicio	1951	Venezuela
José Guillermo Santiago Guzman	1951	Puerto Rico
Raul Lopez	1951	Cuba
Granville "Granny" Gladstone	1951–54	Panama
Guillermo Romero "Memo" Luna	1952–53	Mexico
Lino Doñoso	1954–56	Cuba
Julio Becquer	1955	Cuba
George Bertrand "Bobby" Prescott	1955, 1958–59	Panama
René Gutíerrez "Latigo" Valdés	1956	Cuba
Rudy Regalado	1957–59	United States

Sources: PCL years and country of birth from baseball-reference.com.

Appendix

TABLE 5. PACIFIC COAST LEAGUE PLAYERS OF AFRICAN AMERICAN (NO LATIN) ANCESTRY TO 1959

Name	PCL years	Place of birth
James Edgar "Jimmy" Claxton	1916	Wellington BC
John Franklin "Hoss" Ritchey	1948–51, 1952–55	San Diego CA
Arthur David "Art" "Superman" Pennington	1949	Memphis TN
Alonzo Thomas Perry	1949	Birmingham AL
Parnell L. Woods	1949	Birmingham AL
Luscious "Luke" Easter	1949, 1954	Jonestown MI
Booker Taliaferro McDaniels	1949–50	Morrilton AR
Arthur Lee "Artie" Wilson	1949–57	Jefferson County AL
Leonard Keene	1950 (workout)	Sacramento CA
Harry Leon "Suitcase" Simpson	1950	Atlanta GA
Kenneth Stanley "Kenny" Washington	1950	Los Angeles CA
Walter Loreo "Walt" McCoy	1950, 1951	Los Angeles CA
Marvin "Tex" Williams	1950, 1955	Houston TX
Alphonse Eugene "Al" Smith	1950–51	Kirkwood MO
Eugene Walter "Gene" Baker	1950–53	Davenport IA
Roy Horace "Snookie" Welmaker	1950–53	Atlanta GA
Frank Barnes	1951	Longwood MI
Samuel Harding "Sam" Hairston	1951	Crawford MS
Samuel "Sam" Jones	1951	Stewartsville OH
William Henry "Bill" Powell	1951	Comer GA
Barney Clinton Serrell	1951	Bayou Natchez LA
John Ford Smith	1951 (tryout)	Phoenix AZ
Robert Richard "Bob" Boyd	1951–52	Potts Camp MI

Robert Burns "Bob" Thurman	1951–52, 1957	Wichita KS
Lorenzo "Piper" Davis	1951–57	Piper AL
John Howard "Johnny" Davis	1952	Jackson MS
Edward D. "Stainless" "Ed" Steele	1952	Selma AL
Tom Alston	1952–53	Greensboro NC
Wolferin David "Dave" Mann	1952–53	Berkeley CA
Jehosie "Jay" Heard	1952–55	Athens GA
Milton "Milt" Smith	1952–56, 1959	Columbus GA
Raymond Emmett "Ray" Dandridge	1953	Richmond VA
Curtis Benjamin "Curt" Roberts	1955	Pineland TX
James Buster "Buzz" Clarkson	1955–56	Hopkins SC
R. C. Stevens	1955–59	Moultrie GA
Montford Merrill "Monte" Irwin	1957	Haleburg AL
Marshall Bridges	1957–58	Jackson MI
Lawrence Eugene "Larry" Doby	1959	Camden SC

Sources: PCL years from baseball-reference.com and James A. Riley, *The Biographical Encyclopedia of the Negro Baseball Leagues* (New York: Carroll and Graf, 1994). Place of birth from baseball-reference.com.

NOTES

INTRODUCTION

1. *Organized baseball* is a term used in baseball history to define Major League Baseball and associated Minor Leagues. This definition purposefully excludes amateur, semiprofessional, and the Negro Leagues.
2. "Board of Directors Minutes, 1923–1967," Dobbins Collection, boxes 1–3, California Historical Society.
3. "Board of Directors Minutes, Monday, February 15, 1943," Dobbins Collection, boxes 1–3.
4. "Board of Directors Minutes, June 25–26, 1948," Dobbins Collection, boxes 1–3.
5. Edward Robinson, "Abie's Corner: East-West All Star Classic," *Los Angeles Sentinel*, July 17, 1947.
6. Zuckerman, *Ballparks of the PCL*, 219.
7. "Easter Bunny Brings Coast Crowds and $," *Chicago Defender*, June 11, 1949.
8. Tygiel, *Baseball's Great Experiment*, 248.
9. Spalding, *Pacific Coast League Trivia Book*, 35.
10. Leutzinger, *Lefty O'Doul*; Alexander, *Rogers Hornsby*.
11. Swank, *Echoes from Lane Field*; Dobbins and Twichell, *Nuggets on the Diamond*; Dobbins, *The Grand Minor League*.

1. THE PCL BEFORE WORLD WAR II

1. The agreement also included the American Association, which was a Major League in the nineteenth century and a Minor League in the twentieth century.
2. Seymour, *Baseball: The Golden Age*, 8–9.

3. Essington, "Pacific Coast League," 697–98.

4. The first teams in the Pacific Coast League with a Major League affiliation came in 1932 when the Los Angeles Angels became an affiliate of the Chicago Cubs and the Portland Beavers became an affiliate of the Philadelphia Athletics.

5. Virtue, *South of the Color Barrier*, 37, 59.

6. McKelvey, *Mexican Raiders*, 65.

7. See Van Hyning, *Puerto Rico's Winter League*; Ruck, *Topic of Baseball*; and Echevarría, *Pride of Havana*, 56.

8. Swanson, *When Baseball Went White*.

9. Tygiel, *Baseball's Great Experiment*, 13.

10. Fleitz, *Cap Anson*, 111–12.

11. Peterson, *Only the Ball Was White*, 26–29.

12. Powers-Beck, *American Indian Integration of Baseball*, 177–80.

13. Fleitz, *Louis Sockalexis*. Powers-Beck in *American Indian Integration of Baseball* also mentions James Madison Toy, who played in Cleveland in 1887 and Brooklyn in 1890 (22). During his playing years, Toy did not present himself, nor did others identify him as Native American.

14. Peterson, *Only the Ball Was White*, 54–57.

15. Quoted in Riess, *Touching Base*, 120; Powers-Beck, *American Indian Integration of Baseball*, 68.

16. J. Ritter, *Glory of Their Times*, 172.

17. Following the Amateur Athletic Union, the International Olympic Committee also revoked his amateur status and stripped him of his medals. The ICC restored his two goal medals, though posthumously, in 1983.

18. See Crawford, *All American*.

19. Fuller, *60 Feet Six Inches*, 18.

20. "Barney Joy Is a Husky Chap," *San Francisco Chronicle*, March 8, 1907, 8.

21. Articles in other papers such as the *Washington Post* (December 27, 1906; September 8, 1907), the *Fort Wayne (IN) Sentinel* (September 11, 1907), and the *Connellsville (PA) Daily Courier* (October 20, 1907) printed articles referring to Joy as black, but no such articles appeared in the *San Francisco Chronicle* or *Los Angeles Times*.

22. Franks, *Crossing Sideline, Crossing Cultures*, 63.

23. Franks, *Crossing Sideline, Crossing Cultures*, 63.

24. Goode, *California Baseball*, 215.

25. McNeil, *California Winter League*, 51–57.

26. Wellington is Nanaimo today.

27. Hawthorne, "Rocky Saga," 45.

28. 1870 U.S. Census, Lynchburg (Campbell County) VA; 1891 Census of Canada, Wellington, Vancouver BC.

29. Tom Hawthorne, "Black Pitcher Threw the World a Curve," *Globe and Mail* (Toronto), May 29, 2006.

30. There is the possibility of a fourth child, a daughter born April 16, 1902, in Tacoma, whose birth is recorded but who does not appear in the other census records, so she may have died as a child.

31. 1900 U.S. Census, Tacoma WA. The marginal note clearly indicated a line drawn to John and Emma, but the line indicating James is not clear.

32. 1910 U.S. Census, Tacoma WA; 1920 U.S. Census, Tacoma WA.

33. See Keith Olbermann, "Remembering a Pioneer," *Sports Illustrated*, June 1, 1998.

34. *San Francisco Chronicle*, May 28, 1916.

35. "Angels Win Out in Two Games, Great Excitement in Morning Pastime," *Los Angeles Times*, May 29, 1916; *San Francisco Chronicle*, May 29, 1916.

36. "Police Called as Oak Fans Riot on the Home Grounds—Bonus Champs Lose Twice, Bill Guthrie and a Close Decision Figure in Fight," *San Francisco Chronicle*, May 29, 1916.

37. Steve Corkran, "Claxton Actually Broke Barrier with Oaks, 31 Years before Robinson," *Contra Costa Times* (Walnut Creek CA), April 13, 1997.

38. Bob Dolgan, "Claxton Was Really First 30 Years before Robinson: Mixed-Race Pitcher Played Two Games in the Minors before Rumors He Was Partly Black Led to His Release," *Cleveland Plain Dealer*, September 15, 1997.

39. *Oakland Tribune*, February 20, March 5, 19, 26, April 2, 22, 24, May 7, 8, 14, 1916; "Six Games behind Vernon, Oaks Go after Leaders, Elliott Hoping New Pitchers Will Relieve Young Martin," *Oakland Tribune*, May 15, 1916; "Frank Chance Dons 'Uni' Today in Opening Game, 'Peerless Leader' Brings His Seraphs to Sing for Seals," *Oakland Tribune*, May 16, 1916; *San Francisco Chronicle*, May 24, 1916.

40. Regalado, "'Invisible Baseball,'" 36.

41. Nomura, "Beyond the Playing Field."

42. Franks, *Crossing Sideline, Crossing Cultures*, 53.

43. Franks, *Barnstorming Hawaiian Travelers*.

44. Franks, *Crossing Sideline, Crossing Cultures*, 55.

45. Franks, "Baseball and Racism's Traveling Eye," 187–88.

46. Regalado, "Sport and Community," 133.

47. Franks, *Crossing Sideline, Crossing Cultures*, 55.

48. Regalado, "Baseball along the Columbia," 78.

49. Nagata, "Pride of Lil' Tokio," 103.

50. Regalado, "'Play Ball!'"

51. Feldman, "Baseball behind Barbed Wire"; Regalado, "Incarcerated Sport"; Wrynn, "Recreation and Leisure Pursuits."

52. Vittl, *Chicago Cubs*, 97.

53. Bob Ray, "Portland Club Here to Battle Hollywood," *Los Angeles Times*, May 9, 1933.
54. Bob Ray, "The Sports X-Ray," *Los Angeles Times*, August 18, 1935; "Jimmy Horio to Be Honored," *Los Angeles Times*, August 25, 1935; "It's Tea for Two—and Sacramento's Jimmy Horio," *Los Angeles Times*, September 1, 1935.
55. Spalding, *Sacramento Senators and Solons*, 75.
56. Franks, *Whose Baseball?*, 210; Harry A. Williams, "Japanese Hurler to Make Bow," *Los Angeles Times*, September 14, 1932.
57. Nagata, "First All-Asian Pitching Duel," 13.
58. Harry A. Williams, "Japanese Hurler to Make Bow," *Los Angeles Times*, September 14, 1932.
59. The attempt to attract fans worked. When the Solons played the Angels in September, *Los Angeles Times* reporter Harry Williams estimated that one-third of the crowd of seven thousand was Japanese. Harry A. Williams, "Sheiks Thump Solons Again," *Los Angeles Times*, September 16, 1932.
60. Franks, *Whose Baseball?*, 210–11; "Sports Snickers: Coast Moguls Rekindle Oriental Warfare to Fatten Kitty," *Los Angeles Times*, September 21, 1932.
61. Spalding, *Sacramento Senators and Solons*, 75.
62. Nagata, "First All-Asian Pitching Duel," 14. The article states that it was the Senators who offered Nushida another contract, but I believe the author intended the team to be the Solons since he says "another contract," and there is no previous mention of the Washington Senators in the article, nor did the Senators have an affiliation with the Solons.

2. THE PCL IN THE 1940S

1. Ralph E. Shaffer, "In 1930s, '40s, Art Cohn Fought Sports' Color Line," *San Gabriel (CA) Valley Examiner*, May 8–14, 2008.
2. Chester L. Washington, "Sez Ches: Need of New, Colored Stars in Majors Gets More Acute, but Color Bar Still Stands," *Pittsburgh Courier*, April 24, 1943.
3. Jeff Wilkin, "Back in Time: Remembering Mike and Art," dailygazette.com, March 20, 2008; Jeff Wilkin, "Cohn's California Connection," dailygazette.com, March 26, 2008.
4. Robert R. Kirsch, "Books and People," *Los Angeles Times*, March 30, 1958.
5. "Overloading Blamed in Todd Plane Crash," *Los Angeles Times*, April 18, 1959. Flying on the private plane of Hollywood producer Mike Todd, who was the husband of Elizabeth Taylor, Cohn Todd, a pilot, and a copilot crashed en route from Burbank, California, to New York after the failure of an engine.
6. Libby Clark, "Newsman 'Abie' Robinson Dies on New Year's Day," *Los Angeles Sentinel*, January 10, 2001.

7. Libby Clark, "He 'Fueled' the Engines of Change in Black L.A.: Edward (Abie) Robinson; Renaissance Man/the Ultimate Community Activist," *Los Angeles Sentinel*, February 24, 1999.

8. "Committee to End Jim Crow in Baseball," *Los Angeles Sentinel*, March 6, 1947.

9. "The Fans Can Do the Job," *Los Angeles Sentinel*, March 13, 1947; Edward Robinson, "Abie's Corner," *Los Angeles Sentinel*, July 17, 1947.

10. "'Halley' Harding, Noted Sportswriter, Dies at 56," *Jet*, April 20, 1967, 54; Riley, *Biographical Encyclopedia*, 354.

11. A. S. "Doc" Young, "Grim Reaper Calls Twice," *Chicago Daily Defender*, April 13, 1967.

12. "Herman Hill: USC's First Black Basketball Player Was Activist," *Los Angeles Times*, October 1, 1991.

13. "Herman Hill, Athlete, Journalist, Dead at 85," *Los Angeles Sentinel*, October 3, 1991.

14. "USC's First Black Basketball Player Was Activist."

15. "Negro Leaders Oppose Plan for Segregation," *Los Angeles Times*, January 14, 1944.

16. Herman Hill, "Chi White Sox Reject Race Players: Jackie Robinson and Mate Moreland Barred at Camp," *Pittsburgh Courier*, March 21, 1942; Herman Hill, "'Nate' Moreland May Get Big League Trial," *Pittsburgh Courier*, December 5, 1942.

17. "Negros Ask Try in Coast League," *Oregonian*, October 27, 1945.

18. "PCL to Push Major League Status," *Oregonian*, October 28, 1945.

19. Herman Hill, "West Coast Moguls Adopt 'Wait and See' Policy: Public Opinion Is Key," *Pittsburgh Courier*, November 3, 1945.

20. "Negro Pitcher May Get Tryout with Los Angeles Club of Coast League," *Chicago Defender*, December 12, 1942.

21. McReynolds, "Nate Moreland," *National Pastime*, 55–56.

22. Neither the *Los Angeles Times* nor the *Los Angeles Sentinel* reported about the tryouts with either the Los Angeles Angels or the Oakland Oaks in 1942 or 1943, although Abie Robinson referenced the Angels tryout in an article in 1947. Edward Robinson, "Abie's Corner," *Los Angeles Sentinel*, February 20, 1947.

23. H. Hill, "Chi White Sox Reject Race Players."

24. Saul Halpert, "Hollywood Club 'Too Busy for Negro Stars,'" *Daily Worker*, August 8, 1942.

25. H. Hill, "Moreland May Get Big League Trial."

26. Herman Hill, "Coast Owner Opens Door to All Players, 'Will Give Negro Players Trial on Club,' Says Mogul," *Pittsburgh Courier*, February 6, 1943.

27. Patterson, *Man Who Cried Genocide*, 143.

28. "Wrigley Sees 'Negroes in Big Leagues Soon,' Cubs Owner Says It Has 'Got to Come,'" *Chicago Defender*, December 26, 1942.

29. Patterson, *Man Who Cried Genocide*, 144.

30. Patterson, *Man Who Cried Genocide*, 144.

31. Tony Cooper, "Breaking the PCL Color Barrier," *San Francisco Chronicle*, March 1, 1993, D2.
32. "Coast Owners Refuse Negro Players Tryout, Three Barred after Promise for Try with 'Angels,'" *Pittsburgh Courier*, March 27, 1943.
33. A. S. "Doc" Young, "The Black Sportswriter," *Ebony*, October 1, 1970, 61.
34. Cooper, "Breaking the PCL Color Barrier," D2.
35. Tygiel, "Pioneers of the Pacific Coast League," 10.
36. Herman Hill, "L.A. County Officials Join Baseball Fight: County Board Scores League," *Pittsburgh Courier*, April 10, 1943.
37. "Form 'Fair Practices' Baseball Committee, Plan Program to Force Majors to Drop Race Ban," *Pittsburgh Courier*, May 8, 1943.
38. John McReynolds, "Nate Moreland: Mystery to Historians," *Los Angeles Sentinel*, August 13, 1998, B2.
39. J. Robert Smith, "Coast CIO Joins Fight for Negroes in Major Leagues," *Chicago Defender*, May 15, 1943.
40. Herman Hill, "Pickets Protest Ban on Negro Ball Players, Los Angeles Park Scene of Protest as Pickets March," *Pittsburgh Courier*, May 29, 1943; "Turnstiles Click," *Los Angeles Times*, May 24, 1943; "Picket L.A. Ball Park against Jim Crow," *Chicago Defender*, June 5, 1943.
41. Silber, *Press Box Red*, 1–15.
42. Reisler, *Black Writers/Black Baseball*, 76.
43. Lowenfish, *Branch Rickey*, 363.
44. Paul Meyer, "Columnist Was Baseball Star," *Pittsburgh Post-Gazette*, September 29, 1994.
45. Marvin Williams would integrate the Sacramento Solons of the PCL, and Sam Jethroe would play for five seasons in the PCL.
46. Tygiel, *Baseball's Great Experiment*, 44.
47. The Boston Red Sox would become the last Major League team to integrate, doing so in 1959, a full sixteen years after Jackie Robinson joined the Dodgers.
48. Lowenfish, *Branch Rickey*, 364.
49. Tygiel, *Baseball's Great Experiment*, 42.
50. Lowenfish, *Branch Rickey*, 365–69.
51. Lamb, *Blackout*, 74–75; Michael Marsh, "Writer Helped Robinson Along: Smith Played Key Role in Baseball's Integration," *Chicago Sun-Times*, March 30, 1997.
52. Kleinknecht, "Integration of Baseball." Unless otherwise indicated, the debut dates for the players in 1946 and 1947 come from this article.
53. Bailey, *Junior World Series*, 207–12.
54. A batting average is a statistic that measures the performance of a player's successful batting in baseball. It is the number of hits divided by the number of

at bats. A batting average of .230 is very low, .300 is considered excellent, and .400 or above has been achieved only thirty-five times in organized baseball, the most recently by Ted Williams in 1941.

55. "New Orleanian John Wright, a Pitcher, Also Signed with the Dodgers in 1945, but He Never Made It to the Major Leagues," *New Orleans Times-Picayune*, April 13, 1997.

56. Benjamin Hill, "Forgotten Members of the 'Great Experiment,'" milb.com, February 13, 2007.

57. C. Harris, *Breaking the Ice*, 34–38.

58. McReynolds, "Nate Moreland," *National Pastime*, 60–61.

59. The West Coast Baseball Association was a short-lived Negro League in the West in 1946 with teams in California, Oregon, and Washington.

60. McGreal, "Colonial League a Trail Blazer."

3. JOHN RITCHEY INTEGRATES THE PADRES

1. "Cycle and Arms Team Beat Coast Giants," *San Diego Union*, January 15, 1906; Ed Rogers, "John Ritchey, Catcher," unidentified article, January 17, 1948, in John Ritchey Scrapbook. As noted in the introduction, the Ritchey Scrapbook is an unpaginated collection of mostly newspaper articles gathered by Ritchey and his family about his baseball career. It includes articles from high school through his professional career. Many of the articles are not dated, and most do not include the paper in which the article was printed. I have been able to identify some and have indicated publication details when available.

2. Swank, *Echoes from Lane Field*, 87.

3. L. Harris, "Other Side of the Freeway," iii.

4. Ritchey interview, 9, San Diego Historical Society.

5. L. Harris, "Other Side of the Freeway," 146.

6. Rogers, "John Ritchey, Catcher."

7. Ritchey interview, 5. Bert Ritchey would play football for USC. They signed him not to support desegregation, as he spent most of his time on the bench, but to prevent him from playing on other teams against them.

8. Lapp, *Archy Lee*; Hayden, "Mason's Los Angeles."

9. Berwanger, "'Black Law' Question," 207.

10. J. W. Robinson, *Los Angeles in Civil War Days*.

11. Specified in Section 3 of the Exclusion Law of 1844.

12. McLagan, *Particular Paradise*, 59–60.

13. McLagan, *Particular Paradise*, 187; L. Davis, "History of Blacks in Oregon."

14. Hogg, "Negroes and Their Institutions," 275.

15. Taylor, *In Search of the Racial Frontier*, 122.

16. Some examples include McWilliams, *Brothers under the Skin*; De Graaf, "Negro Migration to Los Angeles"; and Taylor, *Forging of a Black Community* and *In Search of the Racial Frontier*.
17. Jones-Correa, "Racial Restrictive Covenants," 543.
18. McDonald, "Letterbox."
19. Janet Sutter, "Women in the Midst of Things," *San Diego Union*, March 26, 1985.
20. A. Dahleen Glanton, "Blacks Mark Role in Building Country," *San Diego Union*, February 2, 1987.
21. Swank, "Black Balled," 10.
22. Tom Akers column, Ritchey Scrapbook.
23. "Ritchey and Manuel on Prep Team," April 24, 1939, Ritchey Scrapbook.
24. Martin Payne, "Post Six Conceded Edge in Outfield for Coming Series," Ritchey Scrapbook.
25. Will Arey, "Negroes Aid in Local '9's' Late Rally," Ritchey Scrapbook.
26. Tom Akers, "Talking It Over," Ritchey Scrapbook.
27. A. T. White, "Coast Team Is Defeated," Ritchey Scrapbook.
28. Akers, "Talking It Over."
29. "Two Colored Boys Watch from the Dugout," Ritchey Scrapbook.
30. "World Series Opens Tuesday in Albemarle," Ritchey Scrapbook.
31. "Negroes Out as Post Six Club Opens Title Series," Ritchey Scrapbook.
32. "Local Juniors Return Home," Ritchey Scrapbook.
33. "World Series Opens Tuesday in Albemarle."
34. Shaffer, "Cohn Fought Sports' Color Line."
35. Swank, "Black Balled," 10.
36. Wendell Smith, "Ritchey and Am. Giants Major League Prospect," *Pittsburgh Courier*, August 30, 1947, Ritchey Scrapbook.
37. "Batterymen Get Jump on Rest of Baseball Nine," *Aztec* (San Diego State University), February 24, 1942.
38. Bob Lantz, "'Pops' Ritchey Stars at Bat," *Aztec* (San Diego State University), Ritchey Scrapbook.
39. Pat Calland, "Nine Wins Diamond Crown, Dumps Fresno 9-4; 13-4 for First Title," *Aztec* (San Diego State University), April 21, 1942.
40. Rogers, "John Ritchey, Catcher."
41. Strum, *"Mendez v. Westminster,"* 168.
42. Leonard, *Battle for Los Angeles*, 277–93.
43. Swank, "Black Balled," 10.
44. Lydia Ritchey, interview with the author, Chula Vista CA, 2004.
45. Article in Ritchey Scrapbook.
46. Lydia Ritchey, interview in Dobbins, *The Grand Minor League*, 214.
47. W. Smith, "Ritchey of Am. Giants Major League Prospect."

48. "John Ritchey Ready to Join Cubs' Farm in Des Moines," *Chicago Defender*, September 27, 1947.

49. Wendell Smith, "Cubs Try Out Ritchey Negro Youngster," *Pittsburgh Courier*, September 1947.

50. "Negro Backup Given Chicago Cubs Tryout," *New York Amsterdam News*, September 27, 1947.

51. W. Smith, "Cubs Try Out Ritchey Negro Youngster"; Fay Young, "Through the Years," *Chicago Defender*, April 10, 1948.

52. Article in Ritchey Scrapbook.

53. Swank, *Echoes from Lane Field*, 34.

54. Brandes and Swank, *Pacific Coast League Padres*, 29.

55. A. S. "Doc" Young, "Bill Starr, Prexy of Padres, Is Rickey of the Pacific Coast League," *Chicago Defender*, March 4, 1950.

56. Nat Low, "Padres Like Ritchey," Ritchey Scrapbook.

57. Chris Gregg, "Straight from the Shoulder," Ritchey Scrapbook.

58. Swank, "Black Balled," 10.

59. Swank, *Echoes from Lane Field*, 54.

60. Jack Williams, "John Ritchey, 80; 'Johnny Baseball' Was First Black in the PCL," *San Diego Union Tribune*, January 21, 2003.

61. Swank, *Echoes from Lane Field*, 88.

62. Swank, *Echoes from Lane Field*, 29.

63. Swank, *Echoes from Lane Field*, 87.

64. Orenstein, "Void for Vagueness."

4. MOMENTUM AND CHALLENGES

1. Young, *Great Negro Baseball Stars*, 201.

2. A. Young, "Starr, Prexy of Padres."

3. Some affiliations last many years, and some changed each year, which is why the Chicago White Sox are listed twice.

4. Young, *Great Negro Baseball Stars*, 200–201.

5. Young, *Great Negro Baseball Stars*, 201–2.

6. "Luke Easter Helps Draw Record Sunday Crowd at San Francisco," *The Sporting News*, June 1, 1949.

7. Cattau, "So, Maybe There Really Is Such a Thing," 119.

8. Leighton, *America's Growing Pains*, 132.

9. Riley, *Biographical Encyclopedia*, 867.

10. Fullerton, *Every Other Sunday*, 38.

11. Filip Bondy, "Story of a Different Color," *New York Daily News*, September 16, 1993; Bob Dolgan, "He Could Always Hit: Artie Wilson Was the Last Player to Bat .400 in the Negro Leagues," *Cleveland Plain Dealer*, August 26, 1997.

12. Ross Forman, "Negro League Great Artie Wilson Profiled," *Sports Collectors Digest*, January 29, 1993, 76.

13. In Major League Baseball, .400 has been reached thirty-five times. Only thirteen of those occurred after 1900. Ted Williams was the last Major League player to achieve .400, which he did in 1941.

14. Albert B. Chandler, "In re Cleveland–New York Yankees Controversy in Connection with Signing of Players Arthur Lee Wilson and Luis A. Marquez," Arthur Lee Wilson Player File, National Baseball Hall of Fame Library.

15. Wilson was making $750 a month as a Birmingham Black Baron.

16. "Decision Pending in Negro Cases," *Oakland Tribune*, March 4, 1949. A second contract issue between the New York Yankees, the Cleveland Indians, and a Negro League player was also resolved. The Cleveland Indians received the contract of Luis Márquez over the New York Yankees after finding that Márquez did not disclose a 120-day purchase option held by Cleveland when he began negotiations with the Yankees.

17. "Harris Says John Ritchey 'Can't Miss,'" *Los Angeles Times*, February 28, 1949.

18. Miñoso with Fernandez and Kleinfelder, *Extra Innings*, 43.

19. Regalado, "Minor League Experience," 66.

20. Regalado, "Minor League Experience," 66, 67.

21. Miñoso with Fernandez and Kleinfelder, *Extra Innings*, 44.

22. Cooper, "Breaking the PCL Color Barrier," D2.

23. By this point of the 1949 season, San Diego, Oakland, and Portland had integrated. Portland is discussed below.

24. Emmons Byrne, "The Bull Pen," *Oakland Tribune*, March 9, 1949.

25. "Bid for Richardson," *Oakland Tribune*, March 18, 1949.

26. Kelley, *Negro Leagues Revisited*, 175–6.

27. Kelley, *Voices from the Negro Leagues*, 93.

28. Rogosin, *Invisible Men*, 176–77.

29. Luis Angel Márquez Player File, National Baseball Hall of Fame Library.

30. Tygiel, *Baseball's Great Experiment*, 244, 245, 250.

31. "Portland to Get 2 Negro Players," *Portland Oregonian*, May 23, 1949.

32. In 1951 the Boston Braves drafted Márquez to room with Sam Jethroe. Ironically, the color of their skin brought Márquez and Jethroe together, but the difference in the cultural backgrounds was not as similar.

33. Al Wolf, "Haney's Comets Take 5th in Row," *Portland Oregonian*, May 28, 1949.

34. Al Wolf, "Twinks Tumble Beavers, 4–1," *Los Angeles Times*, May 25, 1949.

35. Burgos, *Playing America's Game*, 86.

36. Burgos, *Playing America's Game*, 137.

37. Rogosin, *Invisible Men*, 152–77.

38. Virtue, *South of the Color Barrier*, 88.

39. Virtue, *South of the Color Barrier*, 153.
40. Virtue, *South of the Color Barrier*, 89.
41. Hernández, *Rise of the Latin American Baseball League*.
42. Article by Earl Keller, Ritchey Scrapbook.
43. Article by Keller, Ritchey Scrapbook.
44. Hermann Hill, "Hits Hard in Clutch during First Season," Ritchey Scrapbook.
45. Ritchey Scrapbook.
46. Virtue, *South of the Color Barrier*, 119.
47. Virtue, *South of the Color Barrier*, 93.
48. Regalado, "Minor League Experience," 65.
49. Alamillo, "Peloteros in Paradise"; Balderrama and Santillan, *Mexican American Baseball*; Regalado, "Baseball in the Barrios."
50. Regalado, "'Dodgers Béisbol Is on the Air,'" 282–83.
51. In 1945 Nay Fernandez became the only San Diego Padre killed in World War II.
52. Regalado, "Minor League Experience," 67.
53. Riley, *Biographical Encyclopedia*, 531.
54. Booker J. McDaniels Player File, National Baseball Hall of Fame Library.
55. Holway, *Complete Book*, 392.
56. Heaphy, *Negro Leagues*, 169.
57. "Booker McDaniels Back with Monarchs," *Chicago Defender*, February 26, 1949.
58. Neil Lanctot, *Negro League Baseball*, 348.
59. "McDaniel [*sic*] Bows in for Angels with Five-Hitter," *Los Angeles Times*, June 16, 1949.

5. THE PACIFIC COAST LEAGUE INTEGRATES

1. Russ J. Cowans, "Dozen Negroes in PCL Eyeing Big Time Jobs," *Chicago Defender*, March 31, 1951.
2. Fourteen additional players of color would play on PCL teams from 1953 to 1957.
3. Cooper, "Breaking the PCL Color Barrier," D2.
4. Tygiel, *Baseball's Great Experiment*, 254.
5. Cooper, "Breaking the PCL Color Barrier," D2.
6. Cooper, "Breaking the PCL Color Barrier," D2.
7. Tygiel, *Baseball's Great Experiment*, 255.
8. Tygiel, *Baseball's Great Experiment*, 256–57.
9. Tygiel, *Baseball's Great Experiment*, 248.
10. Tygiel, *Baseball's Great Experiment*, 257.
11. "Players Brawl as Oaks Drop Pair to Seals," *Los Angeles Times*, July 28, 1952.
12. Cooper, "Breaking the PCL Color Barrier," D2.
13. Halley Harding, *Los Angeles Sentinel*, August 10, 1950.
14. "Harris Signed by Padres," *Los Angeles Sentinel*, December 23, 1948.

15. A. S. "Doc" Young, "Artie Wilson: The Birmingham Gentleman," *Chicago Defender*, October 1, 1949.

16. "Rickey Did Not Pull 'Jet' Boner," *Chicago Defender*, July 8, 1950.

17. A. S. "Doc" Young, "Sportivanting," *Los Angeles Sentinel*, February 24, 1949.

18. A. S. "Doc" Young, "Stars Take on Oaks, Seals; ChiSox Call Sam Hairston," *Los Angeles Sentinel*, July 26, 1951; Eddie Burbridge, "Layin' It on the Line," *Los Angeles Sentinel*, March 8, 1956.

19. "N.Y. Giants Ink Monte Irvin and Ford Smith," *Los Angeles Sentinel*, February 3, 1949.

20. Tygiel, *Baseball's Great Experiment*, 104.

21. Brock Brockenbury, "Tying the Score," *Chicago Defender*, November 29, 1956.

22. Kelley, *Negro Leagues Revisited*, 175–76.

23. Frank Austin integrated the Portland Beavers on May 24, 1949. See chapter 4.

24. Kelley, *Negro Leagues Revisited*, 176–77.

25. "Negro Second Baseman Is Signed by White to Bolster Solon's Infield," *Sacramento Bee*, August 24, 1950.

26. Barnes and Elston were the tenth and eleventh player contracts the Kansas City Monarchs sold to the Major Leagues. Jackie Robinson was the first. Russ Cowans, "Russ' Corner," *Chicago Defender*, July 29, 1950.

27. "Baseball Yanks Sign 2 Negroes," *Chicago Defender*, July 29, 1950.

28. Elston Howard would integrate the Yankees on April 14, 1955.

29. Bob Stevens, "It Come Up Mud for S.F., Oaks; Acorn Richard Gets Draft Call," *San Francisco Chronicle*, March 2, 1951.

30. Bob Stevens, "Rain Again Pelts Seals," *San Francisco Chronicle*, March 5, 1951.

31. Bob Stevens, "Bob Thurman Checks In and Impresses O'Doul," *San Francisco Chronicle*, March 6, 1951.

32. Stevens, "Thurman Checks In."

33. Bob Stevens, "Seals vs. Rain," *San Francisco Chronicle*, March 7, 1951.

34. Bob Stevens, "Bucs Clout Seals, 14–5, Acorns Edged by Cubs," *San Francisco Chronicle*, March 17, 1951.

35. Bob Stevens, "Connors' 3 Homers Overpower Seals, 12–1," *San Francisco Chronicle*, April 1, 1951; Al Wolf, "Angels Win as Connors Hits Three Homers," *Los Angeles Times*, April 1, 1951. The *Los Angeles Times* also felt that Chuck Connors should be called the "Pale Luke Easter."

36. "Seals Obtain New Catcher; Peddle Perry," *San Francisco Chronicle*, April 3, 1951.

37. R. V. Tyson, "Negro Players Are Barred by S.F. Seals," *Chicago Defender*, March 7, 1948. As previously mentioned, these players would be given another tryout opportunity in Oakland in 1949.

38. "Seals Sign Negro Hurler," *Chicago Defender*, March 5, 1949.

39. Mednick, "Bonnie Serrell."

40. Mednick, "Bonnie Serrell."

41. Mednick, "Bonnie Serrell."

42. Moe Berg worked for the Office of Strategic Services and used his trips to Japan as an opportunity to take pictures of Tokyo. Dawidoff, *Catcher Was a Spy.*

43. Quoted in Leutzinger, *Lefty O'Doul*, 65.

44. Leutzinger, *Lefty O'Doul*, 53.

45. Al Wolf, "Stars Pitch '50 Baseball Camp: Heavy Overcast Greets Champs at San Fernando," *Los Angeles Times*, February 21, 1950.

46. "Wedemeyer Signs with Yakima Bears," *Los Angeles Times*, March 28, 1950; "Wedey Released by Salt Lake City," *Los Angeles Times*, May 25, 1950. Baseball -reference.com does not include Wedemeyer's time in Yakima. After his career in professional sports, Wedemeyer would become an actor best known for his work on the 1970s television show *Hawaii Five-o.*

47. "Kelly Bids Intrasquad Tilt Today," *Los Angeles Times*, February 26, 1950; "Salt Lake Bees Tip San Jose Nines, 5–3," *Los Angeles Times*, April 10, 1950.

48. Fitts, *Wally Yonamine*, 63–64.

49. Roy Horace Welmaker Player File, National Baseball Hall of Fame Library.

50. Al Wolf, "Cubs Edge Tribe, 3–2, before 24,517 Fans," *Los Angeles Times*, March 21, 1949; "Sharman's Hit Gives Troy Edge over Tribe B's," *Los Angeles Times*, March 21, 1949.

51. Welmaker Player File; Wolf, "Stars Pitch '50 Baseball Camp."

52. Al Wolf, "Padres Sweep Two Games from Angels," *Los Angeles Times*, April 10, 1950; Welmaker Player File.

53. Bob Lantz, "'Bonus Clause' Added to Cesta Stars' Pacts," *Los Angeles Times*, January 16, 1951.

54. "PCL Opens 49th Season; 7 of 8 Clubs Own Negroes," *Los Angeles Sentinel*, March 22, 1951.

55. "Hornsby Checks In at Sud Training Camp," *Los Angeles Times*, February 27, 1951.

56. "Smith Joins Seattle Squad," *Los Angeles Times*, March 7, 1951.

57. "Training Camp Notes," *Los Angeles Sentinel*, March 22, 1951.

58. "Ford Smith, Suds Part Company over Money Matter," *Los Angeles Times*, March 25, 1951.

59. "Ford Smith Quits Seattle Rainiers in Bonus Beef," *Los Angeles Sentinel*, April 5, 1951.

60. Skinner, "John Ford Smith," 13.

61. Raley, *Pitchers of Beer*, 160.

62. Fay Young, "End of Baseball's Jim Crow Seen with Signing of Jackie Robinson," *Chicago Defender*, November 3, 1945; "Negro Fans Plan Boycott of Owens," *Chicago Defender*, August 17, 1946; "Training Camp Notes," *Los Angeles Sentinel*, March 22, 1951.

63. Raley, *Pitchers of Beer*, 160–61.

64. John B. Old, "Hollywood Seventh Club to Add Negro," *The Sporting News*, May 16, 1951.
65. Seattle Rainier Baseball Club Records, Washington State Historical Society. The collection covers 1937–60, and the finding aid describes the material as fragmentary.
66. Briley, "In the Tradition of Jackie Robinson."
67. "Minutes of the Special Meeting of Board of Directors Seattle Rainiers Baseball Club, Inc.," November 26, 1951, 3, Seattle Rainier Baseball Club Records; "Minutes of the Fifteenth Annual Meeting of the Stockholders of Seattle Rainiers Baseball Club, Inc.," April 9, 1952, 4, Seattle Rainier Baseball Club Records.

AFTERWORD

1. Swank, *Echoes from Lane Field*, 88.
2. Kelly House, "Negro League Star and Former Portland Beaver Artie Wilson Has Died at Age 90," oregonlive.com, October 31, 2010; Benjamin Hill, "PCL Legend Wilson Remembered Fondly," milb.com, November 1, 2010.
3. Carlson and Andresen, *The Portland Beavers*, 60.
4. Luis Angel Márquez Player File, National Baseball Hall of Fame Library.
5. "Angels Sell McDaniels," *Pittsburgh Courier*, February 21, 1951.
6. Questionnaire, Player File, National Baseball Hall of Fame Library; Joel Grover, "Roy Welmaker, Pitcher in the Negro National Leagues," *Atlanta Journal-Constitution*, February 7, 1998.
7. "Robert Richard 'Bobby' Boyd," *Wichita Eagle*, September 9, 2004; Bob Rivas, "Bob Boyd," http://sabr.org/bioproj/person/55b9c9fa.

BIBLIOGRAPHY

ARCHIVAL AND MANUSCRIPT SOURCES

California Historical Society, San Francisco

Dobbins, Dick. Collection on the Pacific Coast League, 1866–1999. MS 4031.

McElderry, Stuart. "Boundaries and Limits: Housing Segregation and Civil Rights Activism in Portland, Oregon, 1930–1962." Unpublished paper.

National Baseball Hall of Fame Library, Cooperstown NY

City Files.

O'Neill, Emma. "The Seattle Steelheads: Seattle's Lost Legacy." "Seattle Steelhead" File.

Player Files.

Subject Files.

Team Files.

Oregon Historical Society, Portland

Wood, Thomas Alexander. "The First Admissions of Collored [sic] Children to the Portland Public Schools." Unpublished manuscript, no. 37.

San Diego Historical Society

Ritchey, Bert. Interview by Leonard Knight, April 4, 1985. San Diego Historical Society Oral History Program.

Vertical Files.

Washington State Historical Society, Tacoma

Seattle Rainier Baseball Club Records. MSSC 139, box 4, folder 10.

PUBLISHED SOURCES

Aaron, Hank, and Lonnie Wheeler. *I Had a Hammer: The Hank Aaron Story*. New York: HarperCollins, 1991.

Abbott, Carl. "Regional City and Network City: Portland and Seattle in the Twentieth Century." *Western Historical Quarterly* 23 (August 1992): 293–319.

Abdel-Shehid, Gamal. "Who Da' Man: Black Masculinities and Sport in Canada." PhD diss., York University, 1999.

Adelson, Bruce. *Brushing Back Jim Crow: The Integration of Minor League Baseball in the American South*. Charlottesville: University Press of Virginia, 1999.

Alamillo, José M. "Peloteros in Paradise: Mexican American Baseball and Oppositional Politics in Southern California, 1930–1950." *Western Historical Quarterly* 34, no. 2 (2000): 191–211.

Alexander, Charles C. *Breaking the Slump: Baseball in the Depression Era*. New York: Columbia University Press, 2002.

——. *Our Game: An American Baseball History*. New York: MJF Books, 1991.

——. *Rogers Hornsby: A Biography*. New York: Henry Holt, 1995.

Alvarez, Robert R., Jr. "The Lemon Grove Incident: The Nation's First Successful Desegregation Court Case." *Journal of San Diego History* 32 (Spring 1986): 116–35.

Anderson, Karen Tucker. "Last Hired, First Fired: Black Women Workers during World War II." *Journal of American History* 69 (June 1982): 83–97.

Armour, Mark. *Joe Cronin: A Life in Baseball*. Lincoln: University of Nebraska Press, 2010.

Ashe, Arthur. *A Hard Road to Glory: A History of the African American Athlete*. 3 vols. New York: Warner Books, 1988.

Auerbach, Arnold "Red," and Joe Fitzgerald. *Red Auerbach: An Autobiography*. New York: G. P. Putnam's Sons, 1977.

Bailey, Bob. *History of the Junior World Series*. Lanham MD: Scarecrow Press, 2004.

Baldassaro, Lawrence, and Richard A. Johnson, eds. *The American Game: Baseball and Ethnicity*. Carbondale: Southern Illinois University Press, 2002.

Balderrama, Francisco E., and Richard A. Santillan. *Mexican American Baseball in Los Angeles*. Charleston SC: Arcadia, 2011.

Barzun, Jacques. *God's Country and Mine: A Declaration of Love Spiced with a Few Harsh Words*. Westport CT: Greenwood Press, 1954.

Bay, Mia. *The White Image in the Black Mind: African-American Ideas about White People, 1830–1925*. New York: Oxford University Press, 2000.

Bellson, Ford. "Labor Gains on the Coast: A Report on the Integration of Negro Workers into the Maritime Unions of the Pacific Coast States." *Opportunity: Journal of Negro Life* 17 (May 1939): 142–43.

Bennett, Lerone. *Before the Mayflower: A History of the Negro in America, 1916–1964*. Rev. ed. Baltimore: Penguin Books, 1973.

Berardi, Gayle K., and Thomas W. Segady. "The Development of African-American Newspapers in the American West: A Sociohistorical Perspective." *Journal of Negro History* 75 (Summer–Autumn 1990): 96–111.

Berman, Jay. "The 1956 Los Angeles Angels." *National Pastime* 17 (1977): 81–83.

Berwanger, Eugene H. "The 'Black Law' Question in Ante-bellum California." *Journal of the West* 6 (1967): 205–20.

Beverage, Richard E. *The Angels: Los Angeles in the Pacific Coast League, 1919-1957.* Placentia CA: Deacon Press, 1981.

———. "Casey Stengel and the 1948 Oakland Oaks." *Baseball Research Journal* (1990): 85–88.

———. *The Hollywood Stars.* San Francisco: Arcadia, 2005.

———. *Hollywood Stars: Baseball in Movieland, 1926-1957.* Placentia CA: Deacon Press, 1984.

———. *The Los Angeles Angels of the Pacific Coast League: A History, 1903-1957.* Jefferson NC: McFarland, 2011.

Bishop, Ronald. "A Nod from Destiny: How Sportswriters for White and African-American Newspapers Covered Kenny Washington's Entry into the National Football League." *American Journalism* 19, no. 1 (2002): 81–106.

Bitker, Steve. *The Original San Francisco Giants: The Giants of '58.* Champaign IL: Sport, 2001.

Black, Martha Jo, and Chuck Schoffner. *Joe Black: More than a Dodger.* Chicago: Academy Chicago, 2015.

Blake, Mike. *The Minor Leagues: A Celebration of the Little Show.* New York: Wynwood Press, 1991.

Blee, Kathleen M. *Women of the Klan: Racism and Gender in the 1920s.* Berkeley: University of California Press, 1991.

Brandes, Ray, and Bill Swank. *The Pacific Coast League San Diego Padres.* Vol. 2, *Lane Field: The Later Years, 1947-1957.* San Diego: San Diego Padres and the San Diego Baseball Historical Society, 1997.

Brashler, William. *The Bingo Long Traveling All-Stars and Motor Kings.* Urbana: University of Illinois Press, 1993.

Briley, Ron. "In the Tradition of Jackie Robinson: Ozzie Virgil and the Integration of the Detroit Tigers." In *The Cooperstown Symposium on Baseball and American Culture, 2002,* edited by William M. Simons, 137–53. Jefferson NC: McFarland, 2002.

Bronson, Eric, ed. *Baseball and Philosophy: Thinking Outside the Batter's Box.* Chicago: Open Court, 2004.

Brooks, Roy L. *Integration of Separation: A Strategy for Racial Equality.* Cambridge MA: Harvard University Press, 1996.

Broussard, Albert S. *Black San Francisco: The Struggle for Racial Equality in the West, 1900-1954.* Lawrence: University Press of Kansas, 1993.

Bruce, Janet. *The Kansas City Monarchs: Champions of Black Baseball.* Lawrence: University Press of Kansas, 1985.

Bryant, Howard. *Shut Out: A Story of Race and Baseball in Boston.* New York: Routledge, 2002.

Bunch, Lonnie, III. "A Past Not Necessarily Prologue: The African American in Los Angeles." In *20th Century Los Angeles: Power, Promotion, and Social Conflict,* edited by Norman H. Klein and Martin J. Schiesl. Claremont CA: Regina Books, 1990.

Burgos, Adrian, Jr. *Cuban Star: How One Negro-League Owner Changed the Face of Baseball.* New York: Hill and Wang, 2011.

———. *Playing America's Game: Baseball, Latinos, and the Color Line.* Berkeley: University of California Press, 2007.

Burk, Robert F. *Much More than a Game: Players, Owners, and American Baseball since 1921.* Chapel Hill: University of North Carolina Press, 2001.

———. *Never Just a Game: Players, Owners, and American Baseball to 1920.* Chapel Hill: University of North Carolina Press, 1994.

Campf, Brian. "The Man Who Won Big for Portland." In *Rain Check: Baseball in the Pacific Northwest,* edited by Mark Armour. Cleveland: Society for American Baseball Research, 2006.

Carlson, Kip, and Paul Andresen. *The Portland Beavers.* San Francisco: Arcadia, 2004.

Cattau, Daniel. "So, Maybe There Really Is Such a Thing as 'the Natural.'" *Smithsonian* 22, no. 4 (1991): 117–27.

Caughey, John, and Laree Caughey. *School Segregation on Our Doorstep: The Los Angeles Story.* Los Angeles: Quail Books, 1966.

Chadwick, Bruce. *Baseball's Hometown Teams: The Story of Minor League Baseball.* New York: Abbeville Press, 1994.

Chafe, William H., et al., eds. *Remembering Jim Crow: African Americans Tell about Life in the Segregated South.* New York: New Press, 2001.

Clement, Rufus. "Racial Integration in the Field of Sports." *Journal of Negro Education* 23 (Summer 1954): 222–30.

Coenen, Craig R. *From Sandlots to the Super Bowl: The National Football League, 1920–1967.* Knoxville: University of Tennessee Press, 2005.

Colbert, Robert E. "The Attitude of Older Negro Residents toward Negro Migrants in the Pacific Northwest." *Journal of Negro Education* 15 (Fall 1946): 695–703.

Cole, Olen, Jr. "Black Youth in the National Youth Administration in California, 1935–1943." *Southern California Quarterly* 73 (Winter 1991): 385–402.

Collins, Keith. *Black Los Angeles: The Maturing of the Ghetto, 1940–1950.* Saratoga CA: Century Twenty-One, 1980.

Conmy, Peter Thomas. "Segregation in California." *CTA Journal* (March 1955): 10–12.

Conners, Chuck. *Minor League Baseball Stars.* Vol. 3. Cleveland: Society for American Baseball Research, 1992.

Crawford, Bill. *All American: The Rise and Fall of Jim Thorpe*. Hoboken NJ: John Wiley and Sons, 2005.

Crepeau, Richard C. *Baseball: America's Diamond Mind, 1919–1941*. Lincoln: University of Nebraska Press, 2000.

Crouchett, Lawrence P., Lonnie G. Bunch III, and Martha Kendall Winnacker. *The History of the East Bay Afro-American Community, 1852–1977*. Oakland: Northern California Center for Afro-American History and Life, 1989.

Crow, Dan, and Stephen Sadis. *The Seattle Rainiers*. VHS. Perpetual Motion Pictures, 1999.

Dailey, Jane, Glenda Elizabeth Gilmore, and Bryant Simon, eds. *Jumpin' Jim Crow: Southern Politics from Civil War to Civil Rights*. Princeton NJ: Princeton University Press, 2000.

Daniels, Douglas Henry. *Pioneer Urbanities: A Social and Cultural History of Black San Francisco*. Berkeley: University of California Press, 1990.

Daniels, Stephen M. "The Hollywood Stars." *Baseball Research Journal* 9 (1980): 155–63.

Davis, Lenwood G. "Sources for History of Blacks in Oregon." *Oregon Historical Quarterly* 73 (1972): 196–211.

Davis, Mike. *City of Quartz: Excavating the Future in Los Angeles*. New York: Vintage Books, 1990.

Dawidoff, Nicholas. *The Catcher Was a Spy: The Mysterious Life of Moe Berg*. New York: Pantheon Books, 1994.

De Graaf, Lawrence B. "The City of Black Angels: The Emergence of the Los Angeles Ghetto, 1890–1930." *Pacific Historical Review* 39 (August 1970): 323–52.

———. "Negro Migration to Los Angeles, 1930–1950." PhD diss., University of California, Los Angeles, 1962.

———. "Recognition, Racism, and Reflections on the Writing of Western Black History." *Pacific Historical Review* 44 (February 1975): 22–51.

———. "Significant Steps on an Arduous Path: The Impact of World War II on Discrimination against African Americans in the West." *Journal of the West* 35 (January 1996): 24–33.

De Graaf, Lawrence B., et al., eds. *Seeking El Dorado: African Americans in California*. Los Angeles: Autry Museum of Western Heritage, 2001.

Dobbins, Dick. *The Grand Minor League: An Oral History of the Old Pacific Coast League*. Emeryville CA: Woodford Press, 1999.

Dobbins, Dick, and Jon Twichell. *Nuggets on the Diamond: Professional Baseball in the Bay Area from the Gold Rush to the Present*. San Francisco: Woodford Press, 1994.

Dorinson, Joseph, and Joram Warmund, eds. *Jackie Robinson: Race, Sports, and the American Dream*. Armonk NY: M. E. Sharpe, 1998.

Douglas, Davison M. *Jim Crow Moves North: The Battle over Northern School Segregation, 1865–1954*. New York: Cambridge University Press, 2005.

Dragseth, P. J. *The 1957 San Francisco Seals: End of an Era in the Pacific Coast League.* Jefferson NC: McFarland, 2013.

Dreifort, John E., ed. *Baseball History from Outside the Lines: A Reader.* Lincoln: University of Nebraska Press, 2001.

Droker, Howard Alan. "Seattle Race Relations during the Second World War." *Pacific Northwest Quarterly* 67 (October 1976): 163-74.

Dunkel, Tom. *Color Blind: The Forgotten Team That Broke Baseball's Color Line.* New York: Atlantic Monthly Press, 2013.

Eastman, Ralph. "Central Avenue Blues: The Making of Los Angeles Rhythm and Blues, 1942-1947." *Black Music Research Journal* 9 (Spring 1989): 19-32.

Echevarría, Roberto González. *The Pride of Havana: A History of Cuban Baseball.* New York: Oxford University Press, 1999.

Elias, Robert, ed. *Baseball, and the American Dream: Race, Class, Gender, and the National Pastime.* Armonk NY: M. E. Sharpe, 2001.

Enders, Eric. "The Last .400 Hitter." ericenders.com, September 2000.

Entine, Jon. *Taboo: Why Black Athletes Dominate Sports and Why We Are Afraid to Talk about It.* New York: PublicAffairs, 2000.

Essington, Amy. "Pacific Coast League." In *Sports in America from Colonial Times to the Twenty-First Century: An Encyclopedia,* edited by Steven A. Riess. Armonk NY: M. E. Sharpe, 2011.

Evans, Christopher, and William R. Herzog II. *The Faith of Fifty Million: Baseball, Religion, and American Culture.* Louisville KY: Westminster John Knox Press, 2002.

Fainaru, Steve. *The Duke of Havana: Baseball, Cuba, and the Search for the American Dream.* New York: Villard, 2001.

Farmer, Greene. "Social Implications of Black Professional Baseball in the United States." PhD diss., U.S. International University, 1975.

Feldman, Jay. "Baseball behind Barbed Wire." *National Pastime: A Review of Baseball History* 12, no. 1 (1992): 37-41.

Fisher, James. "The Political Development of the Black Community in California, 1850-1950." *California Historical Quarterly* 50 (September 1971): 256-66.

Fitts, Robert K. *Wally Yonamine: The Man Who Changed Japanese Baseball.* Lincoln: University of Nebraska Press, 2008.

Fitzpatrick, Frank. *In Addition, the Walls Came Tumbling Down: The Basketball Game That Changed American Sports.* Lincoln: University of Nebraska Press, 1999.

Flamming, Douglas. *Bound for Freedom: Black Los Angeles in Jim Crow America.* Berkeley: University of California Press, 2005.

Fleitz, David L. *Cap Anson: The Grand Old Man of Baseball.* Jefferson NC: McFarland, 2005.

———. *Louis Sockalexis.* Jefferson NC: McFarland, 2002.

Franklin, John Hope. *Race and History: Selected Essays, 1938–1988.* Baton Rouge: Louisiana State University Press, 1989.

———. *Racial Equality in America.* Columbia: University of Missouri Press, 1976.

Franklin, John Hope, and Alfred A. J. Moss. *From Slavery to Freedom: A History of African-Americans.* New York: Alfred A. Knopf, 2003.

Franks, Joel S. *Asian Americans and Baseball: A History.* Jefferson NC: McFarland, 2011.

———. *The Barnstorming Hawaiian Travelers: A Multiethnic Baseball Team Tours the Mainland, 1912–1916.* Jefferson NC: McFarland, 2012.

———. "Baseball and Racism's Traveling Eye: The Asian Pacific American Experience." In *The American Game: Baseball and Ethnicity,* edited by Lawrence Baldassaro and Richard A. Johnson, 177–96. Carbondale: Southern Illinois University Press, 2002.

———. *Crossing Sidelines, Crossing Cultures: Sport and Asian Pacific American Cultural Citizenship.* Lanham MD: University Press of America, 2000.

———. *Hawaiian Sports in the Twentieth Century.* Lewiston NY: Edwin Mellen Press, 2002.

———. "Of Heroes and Boors: Early Bay-Area Baseball." *Baseball Research Journal* (1987): 45–47.

———. "Organizing California Baseball, 1859–1893." In *Baseball History 4: An Annual of Original Baseball Research,* edited by Peter Levine. Westport CT: Meckler Books, 1991.

———. "Rube Levy: A San Francisco Shoe Cutter and the Origin of Professional Baseball in California." *California History* 70 (Summer 1991): 174–91.

———. "Whose Baseball? Baseball in Nineteenth Century Multicultural California." *Nine* 4 (Spring 1996): 248–62.

———. *Whose Baseball? The National Pastime and Cultural Diversity in California, 1859–1941.* Lanham MD: Scarecrow Press, 2001.

Frazier, E. Franklin. *The Negro Family in the United States.* Notre Dame IN: University of Notre Dame Press, 2001.

Fredrickson, George M. *The Black Image in the White Mind: The Debate on Afro-American Character and Destiny, 1817–1914.* Hanover NH: Wesleyan University Press, 1971.

———. *Racism: A Short History.* Princeton NJ: Princeton University Press, 2002.

Fuller, Todd. *60 Feet Six Inches and Other Distances from Home: The (Baseball) Life of Mose YellowHorse.* Duluth MN: Holy Cow Press, 2002.

Fullerton, Christopher D. *Every Other Sunday: The Story of the Birmingham Black Barons.* Birmingham AL: R. Boozer Press, 1999.

Garland, Jon, and Michael Rowe. *Racism and Anti-racism in Football.* New York: Palgrave, 2001.

George, Nelson. *Elevating the Game: Black Men and Basketball.* Lincoln: University of Nebraska Press, 1992.

Gerlach, Larry. "Not Quite Ready for Prime Time: Baseball History, 1983–1993." *Journal of Sport History* 21 (Summer 1994): 103–37.

González Echevarría, Luis. *The Pride of Havana: A History of Cuban Baseball*. New York: Oxford University Press, 1999.

Goode, Chris. *California Baseball: From the Pioneers to the Glory Years*. N.p.: lulu.com, 2009.

Goodman, James. *Stories of Scottsboro*. New York: Vintage, 1994.

Groner, Isaac N., and David M. Helfeld. "Race Discrimination in Housing." *Yale Law Journal* 57, no. 3 (1948): 426–58.

Guthrie-Shimizu, Sayuri. *Transpacific Field of Dreams: How Baseball Linked the United States and Japan in Peace and War*. Chapel Hill: University of North Carolina Press, 2012.

Harris, Cecil. *Breaking the Ice: The Black Experience in Professional Hockey*. Toronto: Insomniac Press, 2003.

Harris, Leroy. "The Other Side of the Freeway: A Study of Settlement Patterns of Negroes and Mexican Americans in San Diego, California." PhD diss., Carnegie Mellon University, 1974.

Harris, William H. "Federal Intervention in Union Discrimination: FEPC and West Coast Shipyards during World War II." *Labor History* 23 (Summer 1981): 325–47.

Haws, Robert, ed. *The Age of Segregation: Race Relations in the South, 1890–1945*. Jackson: University Press of Mississippi, 1978.

Hawthorne, Tom. "The Rocky Saga of Vagabond 'Tribesman' Jimmy Claxton." In *Rain Check: Baseball in the Pacific Northwest*, edited by Mark Amour. Cleveland: Society for American Baseball Research, 2006.

Hayden, Dolores. "Biddy Mason's Los Angeles, 1856–1891." *California History* 68, no. 3 (1989): 86–99.

Heaphy, Leslie A. *The Negro Leagues, 1869–1960*. Jefferson NC: McFarland, 2003.

Henig, Adam. *Under One Roof: The Yankees, the Cardinals, and a Doctor's Battle to Integrate Spring Training*. Minneapolis: Wise Ink Creative, 2016.

Hernández, Lou. *The Rise of the Latin American Baseball League, 1947–1961: Cuba, the Dominican Republic, Mexico, Nicaragua, Panama, Puerto Rico, and Venezuela*. Jefferson NC: McFarland, 2011.

Heward, Bill. *Some Are Called Clowns*. New York: Warner Paperback, 1974.

Hirsh, Arnold R. *Making of the Second Ghetto: Race and Housing in Chicago, 1940–1960*. Chicago: University of Chicago Press, 1998.

Hogg, Thomas C. "Negroes and Their Institutions in Oregon." *Phylon* 30, no. 3 (1969): 272–85.

Holway, John. *The Complete Book of Baseball's Negro Leagues: The Other Half of Baseball History*. Fern Park FL: Hastings House, 2001.

———. "Papa Chet, Monarch of Los Angeles: An Interview with Chet Brewer." *Baseball History* 1 (Spring 1986): 52–69.

———. "Piper Davis." In *Baseball History 4: An Annual of Original Baseball Research*, edited by Peter Levine. Westport CT: Meckler Books, 1991.

———. *Voices from Great Black Baseball Leagues*. Rev. ed. New York: Da Capo Press, 1992.

Howard, Elston. *Catching*. Columbia: University of Missouri Press, 1966.

Hutchinson, George. "The Black Athlete's Contribution towards Social Change in the United States." PhD diss., U.S. International University, 1977.

Iber, Jorge, and Samuel O. Regalado, eds. *Mexican Americans and Sports: A Reader on Athletics and Barrio Life*. College Station: Texas A&M University Press, 2007.

Jacobs, Martin, and Jack McGuire. *San Francisco Seals*. San Francisco: Arcadia, 2005.

Jersey, Bill, and Richard Wormser. "Terror and Triumph (1940–1954)." Episode 4 of *The Rise and Fall of Jim Crow*. Quest Productions, 2002.

Johansen, Dorothy O. *Empire of the Columbia: A History of the Pacific Northwest*. 2nd ed. New York: Harper and Row, 1967.

Johnson, Marilynn S. *The Second Gold Rush: Oakland and the East Bay in World War II*. Berkeley: University of California Press, 1993.

Jones-Correa, Michael. "The Origins and Diffusion of Racial Restrictive Covenants." *Political Science Quarterly* 115, no. 4 (2000–2001): 541–68.

Jordan, Winthrop D. *The White Man's Burden: Historical Origins of Racism in the United States*. New York: Oxford University Press, 1974.

Kahn, Roger. *The Era, 1947–1957*. Lincoln: University of Nebraska Press, 1993.

———. *Rickey and Robinson: The True Untold Story of the Integration of Baseball*. New York: Rodale, 2014.

Kashatus, William C. *Jackie and Campy: The Untold Story of Their Rocky Relationship and the Breaking of Baseball's Color Line*. Lincoln: University of Nebraska Press, 2014.

Kelley, Brent P. *"I Will Never Forget": Interviews with 39 Former Negro League Players*. Jefferson NC: McFarland, 2003.

———. "Marvin Williams: One of the Negro Leagues' Greatest Hitters Had Early Look by the Red Sox." *Sports Collector's Digest*, February 19, 1999, 146–47.

———. *The Negro Leagues Revisited: Conversations with 66 More Baseball Heroes*. Jefferson NC: McFarland, 2000.

———. *The San Francisco Seals, 1946–1957*. Jefferson NC: McFarland, 2002.

———. *Voices from the Negro Leagues: Conversations with 52 Baseball Standouts*. Jefferson NC: McFarland, 2000.

King, C. Richard, ed. *Native Athletes in Sport and Society: A Reader*. Lincoln: University of Nebraska Press, 2005.

Klarman, Michael. "How Brown Changed Race Relations: The Backlash Thesis." *Journal of American History* 81 (June 1994): 81–118.

Kleinknecht, Men. "Integration of Baseball after World War II." *Baseball Research Journal* (1983). http://research.sabr.org/journals/integration-of-baseball-after-world-war-ii.

Klink, Bill. "Coast League Dreams." *Sports History* (July 1988): 43–48.

Kluger, R. *Simple Justice: The History of "Brown v. Board of Education" and Black America's Struggle for Equality*. New York: Vintage Books, 1975.

Knight, Michael. "The Oakland Larks." *Oakland Heritage Alliance News* 15 (Winter 1996): 1–3.

Koppett, Leonard. *24 Seconds to Shoot*. Kingston NY: Total Sports Illustrated, 1999.

Kurashige, Scott. *The Shifting Grounds of Race: Black and Japanese Americans in the Making of Multiethnic Los Angeles*. Princeton NJ: Princeton University Press, 2008.

Lalire, Gregory. "Baseball in the West." *Wild West*, June 1, 2011, 34–42.

Lamb, Chris. *Blackout: The Untold Story of Jackie Robinson's First Spring Training*. Lincoln: University of Nebraska Press, 2004.

Lanctot, Neil. *Negro League Baseball: The Rise and Ruin of a Black Institution*. Philadelphia: University of Pennsylvania Press, 2004.

Land, Kenneth C. "Organizing the Boys of Summer: The Evolution of U.S. Minor-League Baseball, 1883–1990." *American Journal of Sociology* 100 (1994): 781–813.

Lapp, Rudolph M. *Afro-Americans in California*. 2nd ed. San Francisco: Boyd and Fraser, 1987.

———. *Archy Lee: A California Fugitive Slave Case*. Berkeley CA: Heydey Books, 2000.

Laslett, John H. M. *Shameful Victory: The Los Angeles Dodgers, the Red Scare, and the Hidden History of Chavez Ravine*. Tucson: University of Arizona Press, 2015.

Lavoie, Steven. "Oakland Pitcher Broke Color Line in 1916 Game." *Northern California Baseball History* (1998): 11.

Leighton, George. *America's Growing Pains: The Romance, Comedy, and Tragedy of Five Great Cities*. New York: Harper and Brothers, 1939.

Lemke-Sasntangelo, Gretchen. *Abiding Courage: African American Migrant Women and the East Bay Community*. Chapel Hill: University of North Carolina Press, 1996.

Leonard, Kevin Allen. *The Battle for Los Angeles: Racial Ideology and World War II*. Albuquerque: University of New Mexico Press, 2006.

Leutzinger, Richard. "Lefty O'Doul and the Development of Japanese Baseball." *National Pastime* (1992): 30–34.

———. *Lefty O'Doul: The Legend That Baseball Nearly Forgot*. Carmel CA: Carmel Bay, 1997.

Levene, Carol. "The Negro in San Francisco." *Common Ground* 9 (Spring 1949): 10–17.

Levine, Leon. *Black Culture and Black Consciousness: Afro-American Folk Thought from Slavery to Freedom*. New York. Oxford University Press, 1977.

———. *Trouble in Mind: Black Southerners in the Age of Jim Crow*. New York: Alfred A. Knopf, 1998.

Levine, Peter. *A. G. Spalding and the Rise of Baseball: The Promise of American Sport.* New York: Oxford University Press, 1985.

Levy, Alan H. *Tackling Jim Crow: Racial Segregation in Professional Football.* Jefferson NC: McFarland, 2003.

Lindberg, Richard. "Miñoso by Any Other Name." *National Pastime* 12 (1992): 55–57.

———. "The 1925 Seals: Place in History." *Baseball Research Journal* (1992): 99–101.

Liscio, Stephanie M. *Integrating Cleveland Baseball: Media Activism, the Integration of the Indians, and the Demise of the Negro League Buckeyes.* Jefferson NC: McFarland, 2010.

Litwack, Leon. *Been in the Storm So Long: The Aftermath of Slavery.* New York: Vintage 1980.

———. *Trouble in Mind: Black Southerners in the Age of Jim Crow.* New York: Alfred A. Knopf, 1998.

Lotchin, R. W. *The Bad City in the Good War: San Francisco, Los Angeles, Oakland, and San Diego.* Bloomington: Indiana University Press, 2003.

Lowenfish, Lee. *Branch Rickey: Baseball's Ferocious Gentleman.* Lincoln: University of Nebraska Press, 2007.

Luke, Bob. *Integrating the Orioles: Baseball and Race in Baltimore.* Jefferson NC: McFarland, 2016.

Mackey, R. Scott. *Barbary Baseball: The Pacific Coast League of the 1920s.* Jefferson NC: McFarland, 1995.

———. "California's Quirky Spurs." *National Pastime: Review of Baseball History* (1992): 23–25.

———. "The California Winter League." *Baseball Research Journal* 24 (1995): 106–7.

Madden, Bill. *1954: The Year Willie Mays and the First Generation of Black Superstars Changed Major League Baseball Forever.* Boston: Da Capo Press, 2014.

Madyun, Gail. "'In the Midst of Things': Rebecca Craft and the Woman's Civic League." *Journal of San Diego History* 34, no.1 (1988). sandiegohistory.org.

Malloy, Jerry, comp. *Sol White's History of Colored Base Ball, with Other Documents on the Early Black Game, 1886–1936.* Lincoln: University of Nebraska Press, 1995.

Marshall, William. *Baseball's Pivotal Era, 1945–1951.* Lexington: University Press of Kentucky, 1999.

Martin, Charles H. "Jim Crow in the Gymnasium: The Integration of College Basketball in the American South." *International Journal of the History of Sport* 10 (April 1993): 68–86.

McBroome, Delores Mason. *Parallel Community: African Americans in California's East Bay, 1850–1963.* New York: Garland, 1993.

McDonald, Louise. "Letterbox." *Crisis* 4, no. 3 (1912): 148.

McGrath, Patrick J., and Terrance K. McGrath. *Bright Star in a Shadowy Sky: The Story of Indian Bob Johnson.* Pittsburgh: Dorrance, 2002.

McGreal, Jim. "Colonial League a Trail Blazer in 1947 Debut: Stamford Team Fielded Six Black Players." *Baseball Research Journal* 13 (1984): 45–48.

McGregor, Robert Kuhn. *A Calculus of Color: The Integration of Baseball's American League*. Jefferson NC: McFarland, 2015.

McKelvey, Richard G. *Mexican Raiders in the Major Leagues: The Pasquel Brothers vs. Organized Baseball, 1946*. Jefferson NC: McFarland, 2006.

McKinley, Michael. *Hockey: A People's History*. Toronto: McClelland and Stewart, 2006.

McLagan, Elizabeth. *A Peculiar Paradise: A History of Blacks in Oregon, 1788–1940*. Portland OR: Georgian Press, 1980.

McMillen, Neil R. *Dark Journey: Black Mississippians in the Age of Jim Crow*. Urbana: University of Illinois Press, 1989.

McNeil, William F. *The California Winter League: America's First Integrated Professional Baseball League*. Jefferson NC: McFarland, 2002.

McReynolds, John. "Nate Moreland: A Mystery to Historians." *National Pastime: A Review of Baseball History* 18 (1998): 55–64.

McWilliams, Carey. *Brothers under the Skin*. Boston: Little, Brown, 1964.

———. *California: The Great Exception*. Berkeley: University of California Press, 1949.

———. "The House on 92nd Street." *Nation*, June 8, 1946, 690–91.

———. "Los Angeles: An Emerging Pattern." *Common Ground* 9 (Spring 1949): 3–10.

Mednick, Barry. "Bonnie Serrell." SABR Lending Library, 2001.

Miller, Patrick B., and David K. Wiggins, eds. *Sport and the Color Line: Black Athletes and Race Relations in Twentieth-Century America*. New York: Routledge, 2004.

Miñoso, Minnie, with Fernando Fernandez and Robert Kleinfelder. *Extra Innings: My Life in Baseball*. Chicago: Regnery Gateway, 1983.

Miñoso, Minnie, with Herb Fagen. *Just Call Me Minnie: My Six Decades in Baseball*. Champaign IL: Sagamore, 1994.

Moffi, Larry, and Jonathan Kronstadt. *Crossing the Line: Black Major Leaguers, 1947–1959*. Iowa City: University of Iowa Press, 2006.

Mohl, Raymond A. "Race and Housing in the Postwar City: An Explosive History." *Journal of the Illinois State Historical Society* 94, no. 1 (2001): 8–30.

Moore, Joseph Thomas. *Pride against Prejudice: The Biography of Larry Doby*. New York: Praeger, 1998.

Moore, Shirley Ann Wilson. *To Place Our Deeds: The African-American Community in Richmond, California, 1910–1963*. Berkeley: University of California Press, 2000.

Myrdal, Gunnar. *An American Dilemma*. Vol. 1, *The Negro Problem and Modern Democracy*. 1944. Reprint, New Brunswick NJ: Transaction, 2002.

Nagata, Yōichi. "The First All-Asian Pitching Duel in Organized Baseball." *Baseball Research Journal* (1992): 13–14.

——. "The Pride of Lil' Tokio: The Los Angeles Nippons Baseball Club, 1926–1941." In *More than a Game: Sport in the Japanese American Community*, edited by Brian Niiya, 100–109. Los Angeles: Japanese American Museum, 2000.

Nakagawa, Kerry Yo. *Japanese American Baseball in California: A History*. Charleston SC: History Press, 2014.

——. *Through a Diamond: 100 Years of Japanese American Baseball*. San Francisco: Rudi, 2001.

Nelson, Kevin. *The Golden Game: The Story of California Baseball*. San Francisco: California Historical Society Press, 2004.

——. "Los Angeles Dodgers vs. San Francisco Giants, April 1958." *California History* 82 (2005): 44–61.

Newby, I. A. *Challenge to the Court: Social Scientists and the Defense of Segregation, 1954–1966*. Baton Rouge: Louisiana State University Press, 1967.

Neyer, Rob. "In Bitter 1903 'War' the Coast Was Always Clear." In *Rain Check: Baseball in the Pacific Northwest*, edited by Mark Armour. Cleveland: Society for American Baseball Research, 2006.

Niiya, Brian, ed. *More than a Game: Sport in the Japanese American Community*. Los Angeles: Japanese American Museum, 2000.

Nomura, Gail M. "Beyond the Playing Field: The Significance of Pre–World II Japanese American Baseball in the Yamina Valley." In *Bearing Dreams, Shaping Visions: Asian Pacific American Perspectives*, edited by Linda A. Revilla et al., 15–31. Pullman: Washington State University Press, 1993.

Normark, Don. *Chávez Ravine, 1949: A Los Angeles Story*. San Francisco: Chronicle Books, 1999.

Norris, Frank. "San Diego Baseball: The Early Years." *Journal of San Diego History* 30, no. 1 (1984): 2–10.

Oakley, J. Ronald. *Baseball's Last Golden Age, 1946–1960: The National Pastime in a Time of Glory and Change*. Jefferson NC: McFarland, 1994.

Obojski, Robert. *Bush League: A Colorful, Factual Account of Minor League Baseball from 1877 to the Present*. New York: Macmillan, 1975.

O'Brian, Robert W., and Lee M. Brooks. "Race Relations in the Pacific Northwest." *Phylon* 7, no. 1 (1946): 21–31.

Odenkirk, James E. *Of Tribes and Tribulations: The Early Decades of the Cleveland Indians*. Jefferson NC: McFarland, 2015.

Omi, Michael, and Howard Winant. *Racial Formation in the United States: From the 1960s to the 1990s*. 2nd ed. New York: Routledge, 1994.

O'Neil, Bill. *The Pacific Coast League, 1903–1988*. Austin TX: Eakin Press, 1990.

Oney, Steve. "The Gene Mauch Story." *California Magazine* 7 (April 1982): 104–8, 153–54.

O'Ree, Willie, with Michael McKinley. *The Autobiography of Willie O'Ree: Hockey's Black Pioneer*. New York: Somerville House, 2000.

Orenstein, Dara. "Void for Vagueness." *Pacific Historical Review* 74, no. 3 (2005): 367–408.

Packard, J. M. *American Nightmare: The History of Jim Crow*. New York: St. Martin's Press, 2002.

Park, Roberta J. "A Decade of the Body: Researching and Writing about the History of Health, Fitness, Exercise and Sport, 1983–1993." *Journal of Sport History* 21 (Spring 1994): 59–82.

Parr, Royse, and Bob Burke. *Allie Reynolds: Super Chief*. Oklahoma City: Oklahoma Heritage Association, 2002.

Parratt, Catriona. "About Turns: Reflecting on Sport History in the 1990s." *Sport History Review* 29 (1998): 4–17.

Patterson, William L. *The Man Who Cried Genocide: An Autobiography*. New York: International, 1971.

Pearce, Ralph M. *From Asahi to Zebras: Japanese American Baseball in San Jose, California*. San Jose CA: Japanese American Museum of San Jose, 2005.

Peterson, Robert W. *Cages to Jump Shots: Pro Basketball's Early Years*. New York: Oxford University Press, 1990.

———. *Only the Ball Was White: A History of Legendary Black Players and All-Black Professional Teams*. 1970. Reprint, New York: Oxford University Press, 1992.

Phylan, Ty. *Darkhorse: The Jimmy Claxton Story*. Amazon Digital Services, 2016.

Pieroth, Doris. "With All Deliberate Caution: School Integration in Seattle, 1954–1968." *Pacific Northwest Quarterly* 73 (April 1982): 50–61.

Pomeroy, Earl. *The Pacific Slope: A History*. Reno: University of Nevada Press, 1991.

Powers-Beck, Jeffrey. *The American Indian Integration of Baseball*. Lincoln: University of Nebraska Press, 2004.

Price, Jim. "A Tale of Four Cities: Pro Baseball in the Northwest Had Its Origins in Seattle, Portland, Tacoma, and Spokane." In *Rain Check: Baseball in the Pacific Northwest*, edited by Mark Armour. Cleveland: Society for American Baseball Research, 2006.

Rader, Benjamin. *American Sports: From the Age of Folk Games to Age of Spectators*. Englewood Cliffs NJ: Prentice Hall, 1983.

———. *Baseball: A History of America's Game*. 2nd ed. Urbana: University of Illinois Press, 2002.

Raley, Dan. *Pitchers of Beer: The Story of the Seattle Rainiers*. Lincoln: University of Nebraska Press, 2011.

Rayl, Susan. "The New York Renaissance Professional Black Basketball Team, 1923–1950." PhD diss., Pennsylvania State University, 1996.

Reaves, Joseph A. *Taking in a Game: A History of Baseball in Asia*. Lincoln: University of Nebraska Press, 2002.

Rebollini, James. *My Heroes: Complete Records of the Pacific Coast League Stars from the '30s, '40s, and '50s.* Sonoma CA: Carneros Press, 2004.

Regalado, Samuel O. "Baseball along the Columbia: The Nisei, Their Community, Their Sport in Northern Oregon." In *Sports Matters: Race, Recreation, and Culture,* edited by John Bloom and Michael Nevin Willard, 75–85. New York: New York University Press, 2002.

———. "Baseball in the Barrios: The Scene in East Los Angeles since World War II." *Baseball History* 1 (Summer 1986): 47–59.

———. "'Dodgers Béisbol Is on the Air': The Development and Impact of the Dodgers Spanish-Language Broadcasts, 1958–1994." In "Mexican Americans in California." Special issue, *California History* 74, no. 3 (1995): 280–89.

———. "Hey Chico! The Latin Identity in Major League Baseball." *Nine* 11, no. 1 (2002): 16–24.

———. "'Image Is Everything': Latin Baseball Players and the United States Press." *Studies in Latin American Pop Culture* 12 (1994): 101–15.

———. "Incarcerated Sport: Nisei Women's Softball and Athletics during Japanese American Internment." *Journal of Sport History* 27, no. 3 (2000): 431–44.

———. "'Invisible Baseball': Japanese Americans and Their Game in the 1930s." In *Baseball in American and America in Baseball,* edited by Donald G. Kyle and Robert B. Fairbanks. College Station: Texas A&M University Press, 2008.

———. "The Latin Quarter in the Major Leagues: Adjustment and Achievement." In *The American Games: Baseball and Ethnicity,* edited by Lawrence Baldassaro and Richard A. Johnson, 162–76. Carbondale: Southern Illinois University Press, 2002.

———. "The Minor League Experience of Latin American Baseball Players in Western Communities." *Journal of the West* (January 1987): 65–70.

———. *Nikkei Baseball: Japanese American Players from Immigration and Internment to the Major Leagues.* Urbana: University of Illinois Press, 2013.

———. "'Play Ball!': Baseball and Seattle's Japanese American Courier League, 1928–1941." *Pacific Northwest Quarterly* 87 (Winter 1995–96): 29–37.

———. "Sport and Community in California's Japanese American 'Yamato Colony,' 1930–1945." *Journal of Sport History* 19 (Summer 1992): 130–43.

———. *Viva Baseball: Latin American Leaguers and Their Special Hunger.* Urbana: University of Illinois Press, 1998.

Reilly, Edward J., ed. *Baseball and American Culture: Across the Diamond.* New York: Haworth Press, 2003.

Reisler, Jim. *Black Writers/Black Baseball: An Anthology of Articles from Black Sportswriters Who Covered the Negro Leagues.* Jefferson NC: McFarland, 1994.

Rhomberg, Chris. *No There There: Race, Class, and Political Community in Oakland.* Berkeley: University of California Press, 2004.

Riess, Steven A. *Sport in Industrial America, 1850-1920*. Wheeling IL: Harlan Davidson, 1995.

———. *Touching Base: Professional Baseball and American Culture in the Progressive Era*. Rev. ed. Urbana: University of Illinois Press, 1999.

Riley, James A. *The Biographical Encyclopedia of the Negro Baseball Leagues*. New York: Carroll and Graf, 1994.

Ritter, John. *The Glory of Their Times: The Story of the Early Days of Baseball Told by the Men Who Played It*. New York: William Morrow, 1984.

Ritter, Lawrence S. *The Story of Baseball*. 3rd ed. New York: Beech Tree, 1999.

Robinson, Jackie. *I Never Had It Made: The Autobiography of Jackie Robinson*. Hopewell NJ: Ecco Press, 1995.

Robinson, John W. *Los Angeles in Civil War Days, 1860-1865*. Norman: University of Oklahoma Press, 1977.

Roediger, David R. *Black on White: Black Writers on What It Means to Be White*. New York: Schocken Books, 1998.

———. *Colored White: Transcending the Racial Past*. Berkeley: University of California Press, 2002.

———. *The Wages of Whiteness: Race and the Making of the American Working Class*. New York: Verso, 1991.

Rogosin, Donn. *Invisible Men: Life in Baseball's Negro Leagues*. New York: Atheneum, 1983.

Rosengarten, Theodore. "Reading the Hops: Recollections of Lorenzo Piper Davis and Negro League Baseball." *Southern Exposure* 5 (1977-78): 62-79.

Ross, Charles. *Outside the Lines: African Americans and the Integration of the National Football League*. New York: New York University Press, 1999.

Rossi, John P. *The National Game: Baseball and American Culture*. Chicago: Ivan R. Dee, 2000.

———. *A Whole New Game: Off the Field Changes in Baseball, 1946-1960*. Jefferson NC: McFarland, 1999.

Ruck, Rob. *The Topic of Baseball: Baseball in the Dominican Republic*. Lincoln: University of Nebraska Press, 1999.

Sammons, Jeffrey. "'Race' and Sport: A Critical, Historical Examination." *Journal of Sport History* 21 (Fall 1994): 203-78.

Santillan, Richard A., Mark A. Oceguega, and Terry A. Cannon. *Mexican American Baseball in the Inland Empire*. Charleston SC: Arcadia, 2011.

Schroeder, W. R. Bill. "The 1934 Los Angeles Angels." *Baseball Research Journal* 6 (1977): 13-16.

Self, Robert O. *American Babylon: Race and the Struggle for Postwar Oakland*. Princeton NJ: Princeton University Press, 2003.

Seymour, Harold. *Baseball: The Early Years.* 1960. Reprint, New York: Oxford University Press, 1989

——. *Baseball: The Golden Age.* 1971. Reprint, New York: Oxford University Press, 1989.

——. *Baseball: The People's Game.* New York: Oxford University Press, 1990.

Sides, Josh. *L.A. City Limits: African American Los Angeles from the Great Depression to the Present.* Berkeley: University of California Press, 2003.

Silber, Irwin. *Press Box Red: The Story of Lester Rodney, the Communist Who Helped Break the Color Line in American Sports.* Philadelphia: Temple University Press, 2003.

Sinclair, Cory D. "The National Basketball Association in Black and White: An Economic Analysis of Consumer Discrimination and Professional Basketball." PhD diss., University of Utah, 2003.

Sitton, Tom, and William Deverell, eds. *Metropolis in the Making: Los Angeles in the 1920s.* Berkeley: University of California Press, 2001.

Skinner, David. "John Ford Smith: Arizona's Black Baseball Pioneer." In *Mining Towns to Major Leagues: A History of Arizona Baseball,* edited by Mike Holden. Cleveland: Society for American Baseball Research, 1999.

Smith, John David. *When Did Southern Segregation Begin?* New York: Bedford / St. Martin's, 2002.

Smith, R. J. *The Great Black Way: L.A. in the 1940s and the Lost African American Renaissance.* New York: PublicAffairs, 2006.

Smurr, J. W. "Jim Crow Out West." In *Historical Essays on Montana and the Northwest: In Honor of Paul C. Phillips,* edited by J. W. Smurr and K. Ross Toole. Helena: Western Press, Historical Society of Montana, 1957.

Snelling, Dennis. *The Greatest Minor League: A History of the Pacific Coast League, 1903-1957.* Jefferson NC: McFarland, 2012.

——. *The Pacific Coast League: A Statistical History, 1903-1957.* Jefferson NC: McFarland, 1995.

Snyder, Brad. *Beyond the Shadows of the Senators: The Untold Story of the Homestead Grays and the Integration of Baseball.* New York: Contemporary Books, 2003.

Society for American Baseball Research. *Minor League Baseball Stars.* Vol. 3. Cleveland: Society for American Baseball Research, 1992.

Soto-Castellanos, Bill. *16th and Bryant: My Life and Education with the San Francisco Seals.* Pinole CA: Clubhouse, 2007.

Spalding, John E. *Always on Sunday: The California Baseball League, 1886-1915.* Manhattan KS: Ag Press, 1992.

——. *Pacific Coast League Date Book: Fifty-Five Seasons of Strange, Silly and Significant Situations, 1983-1957.* San Jose CA: John Spalding, 1997.

——. *Pacific Coast League Trivia Book: Facts about Fabulous Feats and Foolishness, 1903-1957.* San Jose CA: John Spalding, 1997.

——. *Sacramento Senators and Solons: Baseball in California's Capital, 1886 to 1976.* Manhattan KS: Ag Press, 1995.

Stadler, Ken. *The Pacific Coast League: One Man's Memories, 1938-1957.* Los Angeles: Marbek, 1984.

Staples, Bill, Jr. *Kenichi Zenimura: Japanese American Baseball Pioneer.* Jefferson NC: McFarland, 2011.

Starr, Bill. *Clearing the Bases: Baseball Then and Now.* New York: Michael Kesend, 1998.

Stone, Eric. *Wrong Side of the Wall: The Life of Blackie Schwamb, the Greatest Prison Baseball Player of All Time.* Guilford CT: Lyons Press, 2004.

Strum, Philippa. *"Mendez v. Westminster": School Desegregation and Mexican-American Rights.* Lawrence: University Press of Kansas, 2010.

Sugrue, Thomas J. *The Origins of the Urban Crisis: Race and Inequality in Postwar Detroit.* Princeton NJ: Princeton University Press, 1996.

Sullivan, Dean A., ed. *Early Innings: A Documentary History of Baseball, 1825-1908.* Lincoln: University of Nebraska Press, 1995.

——. *Late Innings: A Documentary History of Baseball, 1945-1972.* Lincoln: University of Nebraska Press, 2002.

——. *Middle Innings: A Documentary History of Baseball, 1900-1948.* Lincoln: University of Nebraska Press, 1998.

Sullivan, Neil J. "Baseball and Race: The Limits of Competition." *Journal of Negro History* 83 (1998): 168-77.

——. *The Dodgers Move West.* New York: Oxford University Press, 1987.

——. *The Minors: The Struggles and the Triumph of Baseball's Poor Relation from 1876 to the Present.* New York: St. Martin's Press, 1990.

Swaine, Rick. *The Black Stars Who Made Baseball Whole: The Jackie Robinson Generation in the Major Leagues, 1947-1959.* Jefferson NC: McFarland, 2006.

——. *The Integration of Major League Baseball: A Team by Team History.* Jefferson NC: McFarland, 2009.

Swank, Bill. *Baseball in San Diego: From the Padres to Petco.* San Francisco: Arcadia, 2004.

——. *Baseball in San Diego: From the Plaza to the Padres.* San Francisco: Arcadia, 2005.

——. "Black Balled." *U.S. Athletics Magazine* (2000).

——. *Echoes from Lane Field: A History of the San Diego Padres, 1936-1957.* Paducah KY: Turner, 1999.

——. "This Was Paradise: Voices of the Pacific Coast League Padres, 1936-1958." *Journal of San Diego History* 41 (1995): 3-37.

Swanson, Ryan S. *When Baseball Went White: Reconstruction, Reconciliation, and Dreams of a National Pastime.* Lincoln: University of Nebraska Press, 2014.

Taylor, Quintard. *The Forging of a Black Community: Seattle's Central District from 1870 through the Civil Rights Era.* Seattle: University of Washington Press, 1994.

———. "From Esteban to Rodney King: Five Centuries of African American History in the West." *Montana* 46 (1996): 2–23.

———. "The Great Migration: The Afro-American Communities of Seattle and Portland during the 1940s." *Arizona and the West* 23 (Summer 1981): 109–26.

———. *In Search of the Racial Frontier: African-Americans in the American West*. New York: W. W. Norton, 1998.

Thernstrom, S. *America in Black and White: One Nation, Indivisible*. New York: Simon and Schuster, 1997.

Thomas, Ron. *They Cleared the Lanes: The NBA's Black Pioneers*. Lincoln: University of Nebraska Press, 2002.

Threston, Christopher. *The Integration of Baseball in Philadelphia*. Jefferson NC: McFarland, 2003.

Tuner, Frederick. *When the Boys Came Back: Baseball and 1946*. New York: Henry Holt, 1996.

Tygiel, Jules. *Baseball's Great Experiment: Jackie Robinson and His Legacy*. Rev. ed. New York: Oxford University Press, 1997.

———. *Extra Bases: Reflections on Jackie Robinson, Race, and Baseball History*. Lincoln: University of Nebraska Press, 2002.

———. *Past Time: Baseball as History*. New York: Oxford University Press, 2000.

———. "Pioneers of the Pacific Coast League." *Museum of California History Magazine* (October–November 1989): 10–15.

Tyler, Bruce. "Zoot Suit Culture and the Black Press." *Journal of American Culture* 17 (Summer 1994): 21–33.

Van Hyning, Thomas E. *Puerto Rico's Winter League: A History of Major League Baseball's Launching Pad*. Jefferson NC: McFarland, 1995.

Vermilyea, Natalie. "Kranks' Delight: California Baseball, 1858–1888." *Californians* 8 (March–April 1991): 32–41.

Virtue, John. *South of the Color Barrier: How Jorge Pasquel and the Mexican League Pushed Baseball toward Racial Integration*. Jefferson NC: McFarland, 2008.

Vitti, Jim. *Baseball in Hawaii*. Charleston SC: History Press, 2014.

———. *Chicago Cubs: Baseball on Catalina Island*. Chicago: Arcadia, 2012.

Voigt, David Quentin. *American Baseball*. Vol. 1, *From the Gentleman's Sport to the Commissioner System*. University Park: Pennsylvania State University Press, 1966.

———. *American Baseball*. Vol. 2, *From the Commissioners to the Continental Expansion*. University Park: Pennsylvania State University Press, 1970.

———. *American Baseball*. Vol. 3, *From Postwar Expansion to the Electronic Age*. University Park: Pennsylvania State University Press, 1983.

Waddingham, Gary. *The Seattle Rainiers, 1938-1942*. Seattle: Writers Publishing Service, 1987.

Weaver, Robert C. "Negro Employment in the Aircraft Industry." *Quarterly Journal of Economics* 59 (August 1945): 597–625.

Weintraub, Robert. *The Victory Season: The End of World War II and the Birth of Baseball's Golden Age.* New York: Back Bay Books, 2013.

Weiss, Marc A. "Marking and Financing Home Ownership: Mortgage Lending and Public Policy in the United States, 1918–1989." *Business and Economic History* 18 (1989): 109–18.

Wells, Donald R. *Baseball's Western Front: The Pacific Coast League during World War II.* Jefferson NC: McFarland, 2004.

———. *The Race for the Governor's Cup: The Pacific Coast League Playoffs, 1936–1954.* Jefferson NC: McFarland, 2000.

White, Gaylon H. *The Bilko Athletic Club: The Story of the 1956 Los Angeles Angels.* Lanham MD: Rowman and Littlefield, 2014.

White, G. Edward. *Creating the National Pastime: Baseball Transforms Itself, 1903–1953.* Princeton NJ: Princeton University Press, 1996.

Wiggins, David K. *Glory Bound: Black Athletes in a White America.* Syracuse NY: Syracuse University Press, 1997.

Williamson, Joel. *The Origins of Segregation.* Lexington MA: D. C. Heath, 1968.

Wilson, Lyle Kenai. *Sunday Afternoons at Garfield Park: Seattle's Black Baseball Team, 1911–1951.* Everett WA: Print Shop at the Bend in the River, 1997.

Wilson, Nick C. *Early Latino Players in the United States: Major, Minor, and Negro Leagues, 1901–1949.* Jefferson NC: McFarland, 2005.

Wilson, William Julius. *The Declining Significance of Race: Blacks and Changing American Institutions.* Chicago: University of Chicago Press, 1980.

Wollenberg, Charles. *All Deliberate Speed: Segregation and Exclusion in California Schools, 1855–1975.* Los Angeles: University of California Press, 1978.

Woodward, C. Vann. *The Strange Career of Jim Crow.* 3rd ed. New York: Oxford University Press, 1974.

Wrynn, Alison M. "The Recreation and Leisure Pursuits of Japanese Americans in World War II Internment Camps." In *Ethnicity and Sport in North American History and Culture,* edited by George Eisen and David Wiggins, 117–31. Westport CT: Praeger, 1995.

Young, A. S. "Doc." *Great Negro Baseball Stars and How They Made the Major Leagues.* New York: A. S. Barnes, 1953.

Zang, David W. *Fleet Walker's Divided Heart: The Life of Baseball's First Black Major Leaguer.* Lincoln: University of Nebraska Press, 1995.

Zingg, Paul J., and Mark D. Medeiros. *Runs, Hits, and an Era: The Pacific Coast League, 1903–1958.* Urbana: University of Illinois Press, 1994.

Zuckerman, Larry. *Ballparks of the PCL.* San Diego: Baseball Press Books, 2007.

INDEX

31901063586772

CPSIA information can be obtained
at www.ICGtesting.com
Printed in the USA
LVHW04s0958200418
574193LV00005B/6/P